THE FEDERAL BUREAU OF PRISONS INMATE RELEASE PREPARATION AND TRANSITIONAL REENTRY PROGRAMS

EXECUTIVE SUMMARY

The Federal Bureau of Prisons' (BOP) stated mission is to protect society by confining offenders in the controlled environments of prisons and community-based facilities that are safe, humane, cost-efficient, appropriately secure, and that provide work and other self-improvement opportunities to assist offenders in becoming law-abiding citizens. It is a strategic objective of the BOP to "provide productive work, education, occupational training, and recreational activities which prepare inmates for employment opportunities and a successful reintegration upon release, and which have a clear correctional management purpose which minimizes inmate idleness."[1]

During Fiscal Year (FY) 2000 through FY 2002, the BOP reported that 74,401 federal prison inmates were released from its institutions. It is expected that a large percentage of inmates released will recidivate. Based on the most recent statistics available on federal inmates from the U.S. Department of Justice (DOJ), Bureau of Justice Statistics (BJS), approximately 16 percent of federal inmates released will return to federal prisons within 3 years.[2] Further, according to the most recent study conducted by the BOP on recidivism rates for federal inmates, about 41 percent of federal inmates released to the community in 1987 were rearrested or had their parole revoked within 3 years of release.[3]

According to the DOJ Strategic Plan, since a majority of inmates will be released at some point, it is important for the DOJ to provide them the means to increase their chances for successful reentry into society. The Strategic Plan states that the BOP has a responsibility to offer program opportunities to inmates that provide the skills necessary for successful reentry into society. Therefore, in addition to the basic services (such as

---

[1] The BOP, *State of the Bureau 2002, Accomplishments and Goals*.

[2] The DOJ BJS, *Special Report, Offenders Returning to Federal Prisons, 1986-97*, dated September 2000.

[3] The BOP, *Recidivism Among Federal Prisoners Released in 1987*, dated August 4, 1994.

clothing, food, and access to health care), the BOP provides inmates with a variety of educational, vocational, recreational, religious, and psychological programs. The BOP's inmate programs are geared, ultimately, toward preparing inmates for eventual release.

In addition to programs offered during incarceration designed to prepare inmates for reentry into society (reentry programs), the BOP requires that all eligible inmates receive transitional reentry services through placement in Community Corrections Centers (CCC), also referred to as halfway houses, prior to release. This placement is intended to help inmates adjust to life in the community and find suitable post-release employment.[4]

The DOJ Office of the Inspector General (OIG) conducted this audit to evaluate whether the BOP ensures that federal inmates participate in its programs designed to prepare them for successful reentry into society. The objectives of our audit were to determine whether the BOP ensures that:

- each of the BOP's institutions maximize the number of inmates that complete programs designed to prepare them for reentry into society, including occupational, educational, psychological, and other programs; and

- all eligible inmates are provided the opportunity to transition through a CCC in preparation for reentry into society.

Background

The DOJ is responsible for the detention and incarceration of persons charged with violating federal statutes. The DOJ defines detention as the temporary confinement of individuals and incarceration as the imprisonment of individuals convicted and sentenced for federal crimes. The U.S. Marshals Service and the BOP share the DOJ's detention responsibilities; the incarceration of federal inmates is the sole responsibility of the BOP.

As of November 2003, the BOP consisted of 103 institutions, 6 regional offices, a central office, 2 staff training centers, and 28 community corrections offices. The BOP is currently responsible for the custody and care of approximately 174,000 federal offenders.

---

[4] As of October 2003, the BOP had 6,451 inmates placed in CCCs.

In conducting the audit, we interviewed officials from the BOP Central Office and 3 of the 6 BOP regional offices. We conducted fieldwork or obtained information through questionnaires from 27 institutions. Additionally, we examined reported data for 82 institutions, including the Administrative Maximum Security (ADX) institution, and all Federal Correctional Institutions (FCI), Federal Prison Camps (FPC), and United States Penitentiaries (USP). We excluded Federal Detention Centers (FDC), Federal Medical Centers (FMC), Federal Transfer Centers (FTC), Metropolitan Correctional Centers (MCC), Medical Centers for Federal Prisoners (MCFP), and Metropolitan Detention Centers (MDC) because of the unique missions of these institutions.

Additional information related to our audit objectives, scope, and methodology appears in Appendix III of this report.

Summary of Audit Findings

Research conducted by both governmental and private institutions concludes that successful completion of occupational, educational, psychological, and other programs during an inmate's incarceration leads to both a reduction in recidivism and an increase in post-release employment opportunities. Research in this area also concludes that inmates who transition into the community through a CCC are less likely to recidivate. Therefore, our audit focused on whether the BOP ensures that federal inmates receive the maximum benefit from its programs designed to prepare them for successful reentry into society. Overall, our audit concluded that each BOP institution offers similar types of reentry programs that are generally recognized to reduce recidivism. However, we found that the BOP does not provide assurance that its institutions are maximizing the number of inmates that complete these programs and that all eligible inmates are provided the opportunity to transition through a CCC to help prepare them for reentry into society.

Reentry Program Completions

We reviewed the types of reentry programs offered by the BOP to prepare inmates for successful reentry into society and found that each of the 82 BOP institutions included in our audit offer a full range of occupational, educational, psychological, and other programs that, based on studies, are shown to be effective in helping inmates successfully reenter society. We found that:

- According to BOP officials, the BOP has been working to establish an effective strategic management process for monitoring and evaluating goals and outcomes since 1998 through various initiatives, such as developing program guidelines, directing regions to establish educational goals, and implementing quarterly performance reports. However, the BOP has not yet implemented a standardized process followed by all institutions to establish realistic occupational and educational completion goals. We found that institutions with similar security levels and populations had set very different goals. Further, the program completion goals are stated as the number of completions rather than a percentage of completions. This does not accurately reflect program performance because it does not take into account the effect of the number of enrollments or the total inmate population that could participate in programs, which would allow the BOP to compare performance among its institutions.

- During FY 1999 through FY 2002, 31 to 69 percent of institutions we looked at failed to meet their occupational, General Educational Development (GED), English-as-a-Second Language (ESL), Adult Continuing Education (ACE), or parenting goals. Despite this failure rate, the BOP did not have a mechanism in place to hold institutions accountable for meeting goals. In addition, institutions were not required to develop or implement corrective actions plans to remedy performance and ensure that goals are met in the future.

- The BOP did not routinely review program performance at each of its institutions, despite the fact that there was a wide range in the percentage of inmates successfully completing occupational and GED programs at institutions of the same security level.

- We were unable to analyze trends related to psychological program performance (e.g. completions rates, failure rates, and withdrawal rates) because the BOP only began reporting this data for most of its psychological programs starting in January 2003. Although the BOP has only recently begun reporting monthly participation data, we found that the BOP did not have a standardized process in place among its regions for reviewing program participation at each of its institutions to ensure that institutions maximize program participation.

- One of the expected outcomes of the BOP's Release Preparation Program (RPP), which started in 1996, is that inmate recidivism would be reduced. However, to date the BOP has not conducted any follow-up studies demonstrating that successful participation in its RPP leads to a reduction in recidivism. The BOP also does not track the percentage of inmates that successfully complete the RPP at each of its institutions prior to release.

Community Corrections Centers (CCC)

In addition to reentry programs offered at its institutions, the BOP provides services that assist inmates in transitioning from incarceration into the community. The primary transitional service provided by the BOP is the placement of inmates in CCCs, also known as halfway houses. Prior studies conducted by the BOP have found that CCC placement prior to release increases the chances of an inmate's successful reentry into society. The BOP's strategic plan establishes annual CCC utilization targets for its minimum, low, and medium security institutions.[5] Our audit revealed that the BOP does not assure that all eligible inmates are being transitioned through a CCC. Specifically, we found that:

- The BOP has not established a CCC utilization target for its high security institutions. In our judgment, inmates in high security institutions have the greatest need for transitioning through the controlled CCC environment prior to being released directly into the community.

- According to BOP officials, at each quarterly executive staff meeting CCC utilization rates are reviewed and the regional directors may be required to comment on any utilization rate outliers (institutions with CCC utilization rates that are significantly lower that the target utilization rate). Only one specific security level (minimum, low, medium or high) is addressed at each quarterly meeting. However, we found that during FY 2000 through FY 2002, between 28 and 54 percent of institutions we looked at failed to meet their CCC utilization targets.

- We also found that the CCC utilization targets cannot be used to determine whether all eligible inmates at each institution were released to the community through a CCC, as required by BOP policy.

---

[5] The CCC utilization rate is equal to the number of inmates placed in a CCC prior to release divided by (the total number of inmates placed in a CCC plus total number of inmates released directly into the community). The CCC utilization rate measures the percentage of inmates that transition into the community through the controlled CCC environment as compared to those inmates released directly into the community.

Currently, the CCC utilization targets range from 65 percent for medium security level institutions to 80 percent for minimum security level institutions; therefore, even if an institution achieves or exceeds the CCC utilization target for its security level, the BOP can not assure that all eligible inmates were transitioned through a CCC.

Recommendations

We make thirteen recommendations that focus on specific steps that the BOP should take to maximize the number of inmates that complete its programs designed to prepare inmates for successful reentry into society and to ensure that eligible inmates are transitioned into society through a CCC. Our recommendations include:

- establishing realistic occupational and educational completion goals stated as a percentage of enrollments, and ensuring that institutions are held accountable for meeting occupational and educational goals and outcomes on an annual basis;

- evaluating the performance factors for occupational programs to ensure that institutions are held accountable for low performance;

- developing a suitable measure of literacy program performance and evaluating the percentage of citizen inmates required to participate in the literacy program who have dropped out;

- evaluating participation data for psychological programs and tracking RPP participation to ensure that institutions are held accountable for low performance;

- screening inmates prior to enrollment in occupational programs to ensure that they have the ability and are willing to commit to completing the course; and

- establishing a CCC utilization target for high security institutions and developing a CCC utilization monitoring process that ensures that all eligible inmates are transitioned through a CCC as required by BOP policy.

THE FEDERAL BUREAU OF PRISONS INMATE RELEASE PREPARATION AND TRANSITIONAL REENTRY PROGRAMS

TABLE OF CONTENTS

INTRODUCTION

During Fiscal Year (FY) 2000 through FY 2002, 74,401 inmates were released from federal custody.[6] Based on the most recent statistics available on federal inmates from the Department of Justice (DOJ) Bureau of Justice Statistics (BJS), approximately 16 percent of federal inmates released will return to federal prisons within 3 years.[7] Further, according to the most recent study conducted by the Federal Bureau of Prisons (BOP) on recidivism rates for federal inmates, approximately 41 percent of federal inmates released to the community were rearrested or had their parole revoked within 3 years.[8]

One strategic objective of the BOP is to "provide productive work, education, occupational training, and recreational activities which prepare inmates for employment opportunities and a successful reintegration upon release, and which have a clear correctional management purpose which minimizes inmate idleness."[9]

According to the DOJ Strategic Plan, since a majority of inmates will be released at some point, it is important to provide them the means to increase their chances for successful reentry into society. The Strategic Plan states that the BOP has a responsibility to offer program opportunities to inmates that provide the skills necessary for successful reentry into society. Therefore, in addition to the basic services (such as clothing, food, and access to health care), the BOP provides inmates with educational, vocational, recreational, religious, and psychological programs. The BOP's inmate programs are geared, ultimately, toward preparing inmates for eventual release.

---

[6] The Federal Bureau of Prisons (BOP), _Key Indicators, A Strategic Support System of the Federal Bureau of Prisons_, Volume 14, Number 1, January 2003. The BOP's Key Indicators system provides statistical information related to inmate programs, strategic goals and outcomes, inmate population characteristics, etc., to assist in the management and monitoring of the BOP and its institutions.

[7] The DOJ BJS, _Special Report, Offenders Returning to Federal Prisons, 1986-97_, dated September 2000.

[8] The BOP, _Recidivism Among Federal Prisoners Released in 1987_, dated August 4, 1994.

[9] The BOP, _State of the Bureau 2002, Accomplishments and Goals_.

The DOJ Office of the Inspector General (OIG) conducted this audit to evaluate whether the BOP ensures that federal inmates participate in its programs designed to prepare them for successful reentry into society. The objectives of our audit were to determine whether the BOP ensures that:

- each of the BOP's institutions maximize the number of inmates that complete programs designed to prepare them for reentry into society including occupational, educational, psychological, and other programs; and

- all eligible inmates are provided the opportunity to transition through a Community Correction Center (CCC) in preparation for reentry into society.

In conducting the audit, we interviewed officials from the BOP Central Office and 3 of the 6 BOP regional offices. We conducted fieldwork or obtained information through questionnaires from 27 institutions. Additionally, we examined reported data for 82 institutions including the Administrative Maximum Security (ADX) institution, and all Federal Correctional Institutions (FCI), Federal Prison Camps (FPC), and United States Penitentiaries (USP). We excluded Federal Detention Centers (FDC), Federal Medical Centers (FMC), Federal Transfer Centers (FTC), Metropolitan Correctional Centers (MCC), Medical Centers for Federal Prisoners (MCFP), and Metropolitan Detention Centers (MDC) because of the unique missions of these institutions.

Additional information related to our audit objectives, scope, and methodology appears in Appendix III of this report.

Incarceration and Recidivism Statistics

According to a recent BJS report, as of the end of 2001, approximately 4.3 million U.S. residents were formerly federal, state, and local prison inmates, and an additional 1.3 million are currently confined in prisons.[10] Between 1974 and 2001, the number of U.S. adult residents that had ever served time in prison, including current prison inmates, increased by about 3.8 million.

---

[10] The DOJ BJS, Special Report, *Prevalence of Imprisonment in the U.S. Population, 1974-2001*, dated August 2003.

There are four measures generally accepted for determining recidivism: rearrest, reconviction, resentence, and reconfinement in prison. As a part of our audit, we reviewed government and private studies conducted on recidivism; however, we found no studies on recidivism of federal inmates that are comprehensive and current.[11] The most recent data available from the BJS revealed the following statistics.

- About 61 percent of federal inmates had been convicted of a prior offense, while 39 percent had no previous prison sentence.[12] Of the current federal inmates with prior convictions, 23 percent had current or prior violent convictions, and 38 percent had current or prior nonviolent convictions.

- Additionally, 76 percent of state inmates had been convicted of prior offenses, while 24 percent had no previous prison sentence.

- Approximately 16 percent of federal inmates released to the community will return to federal prisons within 3 years.[13] Information was not available on the number of federal inmates released to the community who were subsequently imprisoned for a state offense.

- The proportion of offenders returning to federal prisons within 3 years increased from 11 percent in 1986 to 19 percent in 1994. Of the offenders returning to prison between 1986 and 1997, 54 percent returned within 1 year of release, 34 percent within 2 years, and 12 percent within 3 years.

- The rate at which federal inmates return to federal prison increases with the amount of time that they served prior to release.[14] Overall,

---

[11] The most recent study on recidivism of federal inmates, the DOJ BJS Special Report *Offenders Returning to Federal Prisons, 1986-97*, dated September 2000, does not include information on federal inmates released to the community who were subsequently imprisoned for a state offense. Further, the study does not contain any information on inmates who were rearrested or reconvicted. The most recent comprehensive study on recidivism rates of federal inmates, the BOP's *Recidivism Among Federal Prisoners Released in 1987*, dated August 4, 1994, was issued 9 years ago and was based on inmates released over 16 years ago.

[12] The DOJ BJS, *Sourcebook of Criminal Justice Statistics*, 2000.

[13] The DOJ BJS, Special Report, *Offenders Returning to Federal Prisons, 1986-97*, dated September 2000.

[14] The DOJ BJS, Special Report, *Offenders Returning to Federal Prisons, 1986-97*, dated September 2000.

14 percent of inmates that served sentences of less than 1 year returned to federal prison, as compared to 25 percent of inmates that served sentences of more than 5 years.

- About 32 percent of federal inmates originally convicted of violent offenses return to federal prison within 3 years of release, as compared to 13 percent of drug offenders.

The most recent BOP study on recidivism rates for federal inmates indicates that about 41 percent of federal inmates released to the community were rearrested or had their parole revoked within 3 years.[15] Of the 41 percent of federal inmates that recidivated, 11 percent were rearrested or had their parole revoked within 6 months after release, and 20 percent within 1 year after release.

This BOP study also identifies the variables that correlate to the likelihood that a federal inmate released to the community will recidivate. Specifically, the major findings of the study concluded that:

- Male and female inmates recidivated at about the same rate. Forty-one percent of male inmates released recidivated, as compared to 40 percent of female inmates.

- Older inmates were less likely to recidivate than younger inmates. Fifteen percent of inmates released that were 55 years of age or older recidivated, as compared to 57 percent of inmates that were 25 years of age or younger.

- Inmates that were employed full time or attended school for at least 6 months within 2 years prior to incarceration were less likely to recidivate than those who did not. Twenty-seven percent of inmates released who were employed full time or attended school for at least 6 months within 2 years prior to incarceration recidivated, as compared to 60 percent of inmates who did not.

- Inmates that were living with a spouse after release were less likely to recidivate than inmates with other living arrangements.

---

[15] The BOP, _Recidivism Among Federal Prisoners Released in 1987_, dated August 4, 1994. It should be noted that federal inmates that are rearrested are not necessarily reincarcerated in federal prisons, which is why the recidivism rate based on rearrest is significantly higher than the recidivism rate based on federal inmates that are reincarcerated in federal prisons.

Twenty percent of inmates released were living with a spouse recidivated, as compared to 48 percent of inmates with other living arrangements.

As demonstrated by the above studies, there are many variables associated with the likelihood that an inmate will recidivate and most of these variables are outside of the BOP's control. Therefore, in our judgment, it becomes important for the BOP to focus its resources and programs on those variables that are within its control while the inmate is in their custody to help decrease an inmate's chance of recidivism. For example, the same BOP study also found a positive correlation between recidivism and actions that relate to some extent to the programs (discussed later in this report) offered by the BOP. Specifically,

- Inmates that successfully completed one or more educational programs every 6 months while incarcerated were less likely to recidivate than inmates who did not participate. Thirty-six percent of inmates released that successfully completed one or more educational programs every 6 months while incarcerated recidivated, as compared to 44 percent of inmates who did not participate.

- Inmates who had arranged for employment prior to release were less likely to recidivate than inmates who did not. Twenty-eight percent of inmates released that had arranged for employment prior to release recidivated, as compared to 54 percent of inmates who did not.

- Inmates transitioned into the community through a CCC were less likely to recidivate than inmates released directly to the community. Thirty-one percent of inmates released that were transitioned into the community through a CCC recidivated, as compared to 51 percent of inmates that were released directly to the community.

As a part of our audit, we reviewed additional studies on the effectiveness of reentry programs to determine the types of programs that are most likely to prepare inmates for successful reentry into society. We compared these studies to the programs offered by the BOP. Based on our comparison, we determined that the BOP offers a full range of occupational, educational, psychological, and other programs that are shown to prepare inmates for successful reentry into society. The studies as they relate to the types of programs offered by the BOP are discussed in the following sections of this report.

BOP Reentry Programs

For FY 2003, the BOP received funding of $216 million for all inmate programs, which equates to about 5 percent of the BOP's $4.5 billion total agency budget.[16] Of the $216 million budgeted for inmate programs, $148 million was designated for reintegration efforts that include occupational and educational programs, psychological support programs, release preparation programs, and other programs that are geared towards preparing inmates for reentry into society and increasing post-release employment opportunities. This amount represents an increase of $23 million (19 percent) of the total BOP reintegration funding from FY 2002.

The following sections provide an overview of each of the reentry programs offered by the BOP and the studies on recidivism that we found are associated with these types of program. Almost all of the studies found a positive correlation between the kind of program offered by the BOP and a reduction in recidivism. It should also be noted that several of the programs offered by the BOP are similar to programs or services that are offered by the community to non-inmates, such as General Educational Development (GED) and English-as-a-Second Language (ESL).

Occupational and Educational Programs

The following studies support a link between occupational and educational programs and successful reentry of inmates upon release into the community.

- **The Practice and Promise of Prison Programming**[17] - The results of this study indicate that the majority of research studies that evaluated prison programming support the hypothesis that inmate participation in occupational and educational programs leads to a reduction in recidivism and an increase in employment opportunities, as shown in the following table.

---

[16] This amount does not include funding for Federal Prison Industries (FPI), which is self funded.

[17] The Urban Institute, Justice Policy Center, *The Practice and Promise of Prison Programming*, dated May 2002.

Occupational Programs
- 9 of 13 studies found participants were less likely to recidivate
- 5 of 7 studies found participants were more likely to be employed after release

Pre-College Education (Elementary/Secondary/GED)
- 9 of 14 studies found participants were less likely to recidivate
- 3 of 4 studies found participants were more likely to be employed after release

College-Level Education
- 10 of 14 studies found an inverse relationship between college education and recidivism
- 3 of 3 studies found participants more likely to be employed after release

Source: The Urban Institute, Justice Policy Center, *The Practice and Promise of Prison Programming*, dated May 2002.

- **PREP: Training Inmates through Industrial Work Participation, and Vocational and Apprenticeship Instruction**[18] - This study was designed to evaluate the impact of prison work experience and occupational and apprenticeship training on an inmate's behavior upon release into the community. The results of this study indicate that prison programs have a positive impact on post-release employment and recidivism. The inmates who worked in prison industries or participated in an occupational or apprenticeship training program were 14 percent more likely to be employed 12 months after release than statistically similar inmates who did not participate. Additionally, inmates who worked in prison industries or participated in an occupational or apprenticeship training program were 35 percent less likely to recidivate within the first 12 months (6.6 percent vs. 10.1 percent). Further, inmates who worked in prison industries were 24 percent less likely to recidivate in the long term (8 to 12 years),

---

[18] The BOP, Office of Research and Evaluation, *PREP: Training Inmates through Industrial Work Participation, and Vocational and Apprenticeship Instruction*, dated September 24, 1996.

and inmates who participated in an occupational or apprenticeship program were 33 percent less likely to recidivate in the long term.

- **Three State Recidivism Study**[19] - The preliminary results of this study support the hypotheses that inmates who participate in educational programs have lower rearrest, reconviction, and reincarceration rates than those offenders that do not participate. The study found that: (1) 48 percent of inmates who participated in educational programs were rearrested, as compared to 57 percent of those who did not participate; (2) 27 percent of inmates who participated in educational programs were reconvicted, as compared to 35 percent of inmates who did not participate; and (3) 22 percent of inmates who participated in educational programs were reincarcerated, as compared to 31 percent of inmates who did not participate.

- **Recidivism Among Federal Prisoners Released in 1987**[20] - This study found that among other characteristics related to recidivism, inmates that successfully completed one or more educational programs every 6 months while incarcerated were less likely to recidivate than inmates who did not participate. Overall, 36 percent of inmates released that successfully completed one or more educational programs every 6 months while incarcerated recidivated, as compared to 44 percent of inmates who did not participate.

- **Prison Education Program Participation and Recidivism: A Test of the Normalization Hypothesis**[21] - This study concludes that there is a three-way relationship between inmate participation in educational programs, the level of education achieved while incarcerated, and recidivism. The study found that a much larger percentage of persons sentenced to federal prisons (43 percent) are in need of a high school degree or equivalent to function adequately in society than the general U.S. population (14 percent). The study also found that 30 percent of inmates who completed an average of 0.5 education courses per each 6 months of confinement recidivated, as compared to 45 percent of inmates who completed no education courses during confinement.

---

[19] The U.S. Department of Education, Office of Correctional Education, *Three State Recidivism Study, Preliminary Summary Report*, dated September 30, 2001.

[20] The BOP, Office of Research and Evaluation, *Recidivism Among Federal Prisoners Released in 1987*, dated August 4, 1994.

[21] The BOP, Office of Research and Evaluation, *Prison Education Program Participation and Recidivism: A Test of the Normalization Hypotheses*, dated May 1995.

We compared the types of reentry programs offered by the BOP with the studies and research noted above and found that the BOP offers a wide range of occupational and educational programs that correspond to the types of activities shown to help prepare inmates for successful reentry into society, as described below.

- **Occupational Programs** – BOP policy requires that each institution provide occupational programs that allow interested inmates the opportunity to obtain marketable skills to enhance employment opportunities after release into the community.[22] These occupational programs also contribute to the operation and maintenance of the BOP institutions. Not all occupational programs are offered at each institution; however, the wide variety of occupational programs offered to inmates by the BOP includes those listed in the following table.

Occupational Programs

• Computer Skills	• Dentistry
• Business Management	• Horticulture and Landscaping
• Computer Aided Drafting	• Barbering and Cosmetology
• Culinary Arts	• Small Appliance Repair
• Housekeeping	• Construction and Carpentry
• Building Maintenance	• Masonry
• Auto and Small Engine Mechanics	• Plumbing, Electrical and Welding

---

- **Federal Prison Industries** – According to the Federal Prison Industries, Inc. (FPI) Annual Report, "It is the mission of the FPI to employ and provide job skills training to the greatest practicable number of inmates confined within the BOP; [and] contribute to the safety and security of our Nation's federal correctional facilities by keeping inmates constructively occupied . . ." In its annual budget the BOP establishes goals for the number of inmates employed by the FPI. During FY 2002, the number of inmates employed by the FPI was 21,778 (13 percent of total BOP inmates), and the goal for FY 2003

---

[22] BOP Program Statement No. 5300.18, *Occupational Education Programs*, dated December 23, 1996.

was 24,788. The FPI includes work skills programs related to the areas listed in the following table.

Federal Prisons Industries Programs and Number of Inmates Employed in FY 2002

Industrial Program	Inmates Employed
Clothing and Textiles	6,665
Electronics	3,171
Fleet Management/ Vehicular Components	1,706
Graphics	930
Industrial Products	1,816
Office Furniture	5,304
Recycling Activities	833
Services	1,020
Customer Service & Support	333
Total	21,778

Source: The BOP FPI, *2002 Annual Report*.

- **Inmate Work Program** – The BOP operates inmate work programs within all of its institutions. BOP policy requires that every medically able inmate will be assigned to a work program and perform work activities that contribute to the operation of the institution.[23] In its annual budget the BOP establishes goals for the percent of medically able inmates that are employed. For FY 2002 and FY 2003, the goal was 100 percent. According to BOP policy, the purpose of the BOP's inmate work programs is to reduce inmate idleness while allowing inmates to improve or develop useful job skills, work habits, and work experience that will assist the inmate in finding employment upon release into the community. The inmate work programs also ensure that the day-to-day tasks associated with operating the institution are completed.

---

[23] BOP Program Statement No. 5251.05, *Inmate Work and Performance Pay*, dated December 7, 1998.

- **Literacy Program** - Individuals without a basic level of education frequently encounter serious difficulty in obtaining employment. Therefore, the BOP requires that each inmate should have the opportunity to complete a literacy program leading to a GED certificate and/or high school diploma.[24] The intent of this policy is to provide inmates with the basic literacy skills necessary to compete for employment.

- **English-as-a-Second Language Program** - Pursuant to federal statute, limited English proficient inmates confined in federal institutions are required to attend an ESL program until they can function at the equivalent of the eighth-grade level on a nationally recognized education achievement test.[25] The BOP also requires that inmates with limited English proficiency skills will be afforded the opportunity to enhance their communication skills through its ESL programs.[26]

- **Adult Continuing Education Programs** – The BOP offers a variety of Adult Continuing Education (ACE) programs in formal instructional classes that provide inmates with learning in areas that may be of special interest. Inmates rather than education staff members teach many ACE courses, which enables the BOP to offer a large number of these courses. The type of ACE programs offered to inmates by the BOP includes those listed in the table on the following page.

---

[24] BOP Program Statement No. 5300.21, *Education, Training and Leisure Time Program Standards*, dated February 18, 2002.

[25] The Crime Control Act of 1990, codified in 18 U.S.C § 3624 (f).

[26] BOP Program Statement No. 5350.24, *English-as-a-Second Language Program*, dated July 24, 1997.

Adult Continuing Education Programs	
• Foreign Languages	• Chess
• Mathematics	• Motivation
• Commercial Drivers License	• Cardiopulmonary Resuscitation (CPR)
• Writing	• Typing
• Finance	• Sign Language
• History	• Floral Design
• Legal Research	• Health
• Literature	• Life Skills
• Public Speaking	• Time Management

- **Postsecondary Education Programs** – Postsecondary education programs generally include correspondence courses provided through junior or community colleges, 4-year colleges and universities, and postsecondary vocational or technical schools. Inmates are expected to pay the tuition for these postsecondary programs from personal funds or other sources such as scholarship awards provided through FPI programs.

- **Parenting Program** – The BOP requires that parenting programs be provided in all institutions.[27] The BOP parenting programs are expected to promote and reinforce positive relationships, family values, and mutual support among inmates and their spouses that may be sustained after the inmate is released into the community.

Psychological Programs

In addition to occupational and educational programs, BOP policy requires that psychology services within each institution be sufficient to ensure that every inmate with a documented need or interest in psychological treatment has access to a level of care comparable to that

---

[27] BOP Program Statement No. 5355.03, *Parenting Program Standards*, dated January 20, 1995.

offered in the community.[28] Through its psychology services, the BOP seeks to create an environment where inmates can develop habits and skills that will make them more productive members of society upon release to the community.

According to the BOP, the main priority of the BOP's psychology services is acute crisis intervention. However, the BOP also provides counseling services, including individual or group treatment. At a minimum, a psychology services staff member must screen all inmates entering into a BOP institution within 14 days (30 days for transferred inmates). Additionally, the BOP offers the following psychological programs.

- **Drug Abuse Education Program** – This program provides inmates with specific instruction on the risks involved with drug use and abuse, and presents strategies toward living a drug free lifestyle while introducing the inmate to the concepts of drug treatment and motivating the inmate to enter and participate in the BOP's Residential Drug Abuse Treatment Program.

- **Residential Drug Abuse Treatment Program** – This program is designed for intensive drug abuse treatment. Inmates are housed separately in residential drug abuse treatment units for up to 12 months. The specialized drug units provide extensive assessment, treatment planning, and individual and group counseling.

- **Non-Residential Drug Abuse Treatment Program** – This program consists of both group and individual therapy delivered through the psychology services department in each institution. This program offers flexibility to inmates who are not eligible for or do not choose to enter the BOP's Residential Drug Abuse Treatment Program. Non-residential treatment services are also provided as a follow-up to the BOP's Residential Drug Abuse Treatment Program while inmates are awaiting release.

- **Transitional Drug Abuse Treatment Program** – This program was developed for successful Residential Drug Abuse Treatment Program graduates who are released to the community under BOP custody. The continuation of treatment, through community-based drug treatment, is required of these inmates during their transition back

---

[28] BOP Program Statement No. 5310.12, *Psychology Services Manual*, dated August 30, 1993.

into society. Additionally, the community transition program now accepts inmates who have not participated in a Residential Drug Abuse Treatment Program but have later been identified to be in need of drug abuse treatment.

- **Sex Offender Management Plan** – The Sex Offender Management Plan is a comprehensive management strategy for all sex offenders incarcerated in BOP institutions. The purpose of the program is to increase institution security and ensure effective transition of inmates into the community.

- **Sex Offender Treatment Program** – The Sex Offender Treatment Program is a residential program offered at FCI Butner to help sex offenders manage their sexual deviance in order to reduce recidivism. The program is based on the notion that, while there is probably no permanent cure, criminal sexual behavior can be effectively managed in most cases through a combination of treatment and intensive supervision.

- **Challenge, Opportunity, Discipline and Ethics (CODE) Program** – The CODE program is a residential treatment program offered in high security institutions designed for inmates whose psychological distress, mental illness or neurocognitive deficits interfere with the inmate's ability to adjust satisfactorily to incarceration. The program is designed to teach inmates basic core values such as respect for self and others, responsibility for personal actions, honesty in relationships with others, and tolerance towards the actions of others.

- **E-CODE Program** – The E-CODE program is an intensive, multi-phase, non-residential and residential treatment program for maximum security inmates. The purpose of the program is to teach inmates self-discipline, the value of conforming to pro-social lifestyles, and changing negative thoughts and behaviors that lead to incarceration-related problems. The program is designed to manage and treat violent and predatory inmates housed at USP Marion.

- **Impulsive-Aggressive CODE Pilot** – The Impulsive-Aggressive CODE Pilot is a residential program designed to identify inmates with impulsive-aggressive disorders and to provide effective treatment and management to reduce their maladaptive behavior.

- **Bureau Responsibility and Values Enhancement Program (BRAVE)** – The BRAVE program was established in response to the BOP's research which revealed that medium security inmates 30 years old or younger have the greatest difficulty adapting to institution rules. The goals of the BRAVE program are to: (1) assist in the adjustment of medium security inmates entering the BOP custody for the first time; (2) improve institutional adjustment and reduce incidents of misconduct through organized activities that promote positive behavior; and (3) identify psychological disorders that may contribute to criminal activity and poor institutional adjustment, and provide appropriate clinical intervention.

- **Skills Program** – The Skills Program is a specialized treatment program for inmates that have significant learning and social functioning deficits. The Skills Program is a cooperative working arrangement between unit, education, recreation, and psychology staff. The primary program components include: (1) assessment and orientation, (2) intensive treatment that includes relational, academic, and wellness skill building, and (3) transitional planning. Additionally, the Skills Program includes the use of well-screened inmate mentors.

- **New Pathways Program** – The New Pathways Program was established in response to research concluding that many women with criminal and substance histories also have a history of sexual, psychological and/or physical abuse, either as children or adults. The objectives of the New Pathways Program are to treat the trauma resulting from sexual, psychological, or physical abuse and to assist female inmates in developing the skills that will lead to independence and healthy decision making.

The following studies support a link between the BOP's psychological programs, inmate misconduct, and successful reentry of inmates into the community.

- **Triad Drug Treatment Evaluation Project, Final Report of Three-Year Outcomes**[29] - This report is based on inmates who had been released from BOP custody for 3 years. The report revealed that male inmates who completed the Residential Drug Abuse Treatment Program and had been released to the community for a minimum of

---

[29] The BOP, *Triad Drug Treatment Evaluation Project, Final Report of Three-Year Outcomes*, dated September 2000.

3 years were 16 percent less likely to be rearrested and use drugs than those inmates who had not received treatment. Female inmates who completed the Residential Drug Abuse Treatment Program and had been released to the community for a minimum of 3 years were 18 percent less likely to be rearrested, and 17 percent less likely to use drugs, than those inmates who had not received treatment.

- **Technical Report for Preliminary Results From the Evaluation of the Beckley Responsibility and Values Enforcement (BRAVE) Program**[30] - The major finding of this evaluation was that inmates who participated in the BRAVE program had substantially lower rates of misconduct when compared to all other inmates who met the criteria used to select participants for the program that were incarcerated in the BOP during the same time period. The study found that inmates who participated in the BRAVE program, overall, had an average misconduct rate that was 26 percent lower than the comparison group. The study concluded that since inmates are directly designated into the BRAVE program upon incarceration, the lower misconduct rate could be attributed to the program itself.

  The study also found that 87 percent of the inmates successfully completed the program and the rate of misconduct among inmates successfully completing the program was 55 percent lower than the comparison group.

- **Misconduct Rates by Drug Abuse Program (DAP) graduates in USPs**[31] - This review of misconduct rates among DAP graduates revealed a substantial decline in the rate of misconduct among USP inmates after graduation. Overall, the rate of misconduct among these inmates was 49 percent lower after they had graduated from DAP. For these inmates, the rate of violent offenses was reduced by 46 to 54 percent depending on the level of offense, the rate of drug offenses was reduced by 57 percent, the rate of alcohol offenses was reduced by 35 percent, the rate of refusal/insubordination offenses was reduced by 55 percent, and the rate of other offenses was reduced by 44 percent.

---

[30] The BOP, Office of Research and Evaluation, *Technical Report for Preliminary Results from the Evaluation of the Beckley Responsibility and Values Enhancement (BRAVE) Program,* (not dated).

[31] The BOP, Office of Research and Evaluation, memorandum, *Misconduct rates by DAP graduates in USPs,* dated October 8, 1996.

Release Preparation Program

To prepare inmates for final release into the community, the BOP implemented the Release Preparation Program (RPP).[32] The purpose of the RPP is to provide inmates with the basic information and contacts necessary for successful reentry into society and the work force. The BOP requires each institution to have a RPP for all sentenced inmates reentering into the community, with the exception of administrative maximum security institutions. Each institution is responsible for developing the curriculum for its RPP to suit the specific needs of its inmates. However, the RPP must be based on core topics and include courses for each of the following six broad categories: (1) health and nutrition, (2) employment, (3) personal finance and consumer skills, (4) information and community resources, (5) release requirements and procedures, and (6) personal growth and development. BOP policy requires that eligible inmates enroll in the RPP no later than 30 months prior to release to the community or a CCC.

The expected results of the RPP are that:

- inmates will participate in the RPP to enhance their chances for successful reintegration into society;

- the BOP will provide releasing inmates with information, programs, and services by entering into partnerships with private industry, other federal agencies, community services providers, and CCCs; and

- inmate recidivism will be reduced through participation in the RPP and contact with community resources.

All sentenced inmates committed to BOP custody are required to participate in the RPP except those: (1) committed for study and observation; (2) committed to the BOP serving a sentence of 6 months or less; (3) committed to the BOP with a sentence of "death"; (4) confined in an administrative maximum security institution; or (5) deportable aliens.

The BOP requires that its unit staff strongly encourage and support inmate participation in the institution's RPP. Inmates who refuse to participate in the RPP are considered to lack the responsibility necessary for

---

[32] BOP Program Statement No. 5325.06, *Release Preparation Program*, dated March 4, 2002.

CCC placement and will not ordinarily participate in these types of community-based programs.

The BOP has not conducted any studies related to successful participation in its RPP and recidivism.

Inmate Placement Program

The BOP's Inmate Placement Program was established because many inmates do not have basic skills necessary to secure and retain employment after release. Many BOP institutions hold mock job fairs at which inmates are interviewed by recruiters from real companies. The mock job fairs assist inmates in developing interviewing skills. The Inmate Placement Program also assists inmates in preparing employment portfolios that include a resume, education certificates, diplomas, transcripts, and other documents necessary for employment.

The BOP contracted for three studies of its mock job fairs conducted at FCI Terminal Island, FPC Phoenix, and FCI Big Spring.[33] All three studies generally concluded that inmate participation in mock job fairs:
(1) increased their awareness of employment opportunities that are available to them upon release into the community, (2) provided them with tools to assist them in finding employment upon release into the community, and (3) increased their self-confidence and self-esteem. The studies also concluded that after participating in the mock job fairs, employers perceived inmates as confident, motivated, and employable, rather than as "ex-cons" and "felons."

The BOP Inmate Placement Program Branch also conducted surveys related to inmates that participated in mock job fairs prior to their release. The surveys were conducted by sending questionnaires to the probation officers of inmates that had participated in a mock job fair during incarceration. The BOP survey results revealed that as of June 2001, 69 percent of inmates had jobs with an average monthly income of $1,288, and only 7 percent of inmates had been reincarcerated. The second year study revealed that as of May 2002, 61 percent of the inmates had jobs with an average monthly income of $1,552, and again only 7 percent of inmates

---

[33] Workplace Learning Resource Center, *First Annual Mock Job Fair, "Gateway to Success, Federal Correctional Institution Terminal Island*, dated December 15, 1998; Development Systems Corporation, *Mock Job Fair, FCI Big Spring*, dated May 17, 1999; and Development Systems Corporation, *Mock Job Fair, FPC Phoenix*, dated May 26, 1999.

had been reincarcerated. The surveys of inmates participating in mock job fairs do not include an scientific correlation between inmate participation in mock job fairs and post-release employment. Further, the surveys do not include a comparison group consisting of inmates who did not participate in a mock job fair during incarceration.

Faith-Based Programs

One BOP Strategic Objective is to "ensure reasonable accommodations exist for all recognized faith groups."[34] Further, BOP policy requires its institutions to provide inmates of all faith groups with reasonable and equitable opportunities to pursue religious beliefs and practices, within the constraints of budgetary limitations and consistent with the security level and orderly operation of the institution.[35] The BOP provides religious services and meeting times for numerous faith groups. Inmates can also participate in self-improvement forums such as scripture study and religious workshops. Additionally, the BOP also offers the following residential faith-based program.

- **Life Connections Program** – The BOP recently established the Life Connections Program. According to the BOP, the purpose of the program is to foster personal growth and responsibility, and to use the inmate's faith commitment "to bring reconciliation and restoration to the relationship among the victim, inmate, and the community." Additionally, inmates are connected with faith-based support groups in the community in which they will be released. The program goals are to change behavior, improve adjustment to incarceration, and reduce recidivism. The BOP has established a FY 2003 goal of 545 inmates participating in a Life Connections program in its budget.

Recreational Programs

BOP policy requires its institutions to encourage inmates to use their leisure time effectively by offering a variety of activities, including sports,

---

[34] The BOP, *State of the Bureau 2002, Accomplishments and Goals*.

[35] BOP Program Statement No. 5360.08, *Religious Beliefs and Practices*, dated May 25, 2001.

wellness, arts, and hobby crafts.[36] The expected results of offering recreational activities to inmates are that the programs will: (1) keep inmates occupied and reduce idleness; (2) enhance the physical, emotional, and social well being of inmates; (3) encourage and assist inmates in adopting healthy lifestyles through participation in physical fitness and health education programs; and (4) decrease the need for inmate medical treatment.

Community Corrections Centers (CCC)

In addition to programs offered at its institutions, the BOP provides services that assist inmates in transitioning from incarceration into the community. The primary transitional service is the placement of inmates in CCCs, also known as halfway houses. BOP policy requires that eligible inmates should be released to the community through a CCC, unless there is some impediment outlined by the BOP.[37]

According to the BOP, during the transitional period at a CCC inmate activities are closely monitored while inmates are provided with a suitable residence, structured programs, job placement, and counseling. Further, all CCCs offer drug testing and counseling for alcohol and drug-related problems. During their stay, inmates are required to pay a subsistence charge to defer the cost of their confinement in a CCC (25 percent of their gross income, not to exceed the average daily cost of their CCC placement).

We found that the following studies support a link between the BOP's transitional services offered through CCC placement and recidivism.

- **PREP: Training Inmates through Industrial Work Participation, and Vocational and Apprenticeship Instruction**[38] - The results of this study indicate a link between inmates who transition into the community through the BOP's CCC placement program and post-release employment. The study found that 87 percent of inmates

---

[36] BOP Program Statement No. 5370.10, *Recreation Programs, Inmate*, dated February 23, 2000.

[37] BOP Program Statement No. 7310.04, *Community Corrections Center (CCC) Utilization and Transfer Procedure*, dated December 16, 1998.

[38] The BOP, Office of Research and Evaluation, *PREP: Training Inmates through Industrial Work Participation, and Vocational and Apprenticeship Instruction*, dated September 24, 1996.

who transitioned into the community through a CCC achieved full-time employment, as compared to 62 percent of inmates who were released directly into the community. Further, an additional 9 percent of inmates who transitioned into the community through a CCC achieved day labor, as compared to 1 percent of inmates who were released directly into the community.

- **Recidivism Among Federal Prisoners Released in 1987**[39] - This study found that among other characteristics related to recidivism, inmates transitioned into the community through a CCC were less likely to recidivate than inmates released directly to the community. Thirty-one percent of inmates that were transitioned into the community through a CCC recidivated, as compared to 51 percent of inmates that were released directly to the community.

Release Planning

The BOP has implemented a unit management concept to manage and encourage inmate participation in its reentry programs. Under the unit management concept, multi-discipline unit teams determine an inmate's program needs and monitor the inmate's participation in programs that encourage pro-social behaviors that benefit the inmates, staff, and the community. The unit teams make decisions concerning supervision, work assignments, and programming for the inmate, and at a minimum include the unit manager, a case manager, and a counselor. Additionally, an education advisor and psychology services representative are generally members of the teams.

The BOP requires that each newly committed inmate be scheduled for an initial classification within 4 weeks of the inmate's arrival at the institution. The initial classification occurs at a meeting with the unit team, at which time the preliminary release preparation needs of the inmate are assessed and the preparation of federal inmates for reentry into society begins.

In preparation for the initial classification, the BOP requires the unit team to prepare a program review report. This report ordinarily includes information on the apparent needs of the inmate and offers a correctional

---

[39] The BOP, Office of Research and Evaluation, *Recidivism Among Federal Prisoners Released in 1987*, dated August 4, 1994.

program designed to meet those needs. In our review of inmate case files, we found that generally the inmate's initial classification program review report includes information on: (1) work requirements, (2) RPP requirements, (3) educational and occupational program requirements, and (4) CCC recommendations. According to BOP policy, the correctional program plans are required to be stated in measurable terms, establishing time limits, performance levels, and specific expected program accomplishments.

The primary source of data used to determine inmate's needs at the time of initial classification is the Presentence Investigation Report prepared by the U.S. Probation Office. The Presentence Investigation Report includes information related to the inmate's: (1) criminal history, (2) substance abuse, (3) education, (4) vocational skills, and (5) employment history.

According to the BOP, release planning and preparation begins with the initial classification and is reassessed throughout confinement during program reviews conducted by the unit team. The unit team is required to conduct a program review for each inmate at least once every 180 days. Further, the unit team is required to conduct a program review at least every 90 days when an inmate is within 12 months of the inmate's projected release date. At the time of the program review, the unit team also prepares a report that documents the inmate's progress toward expected program accomplishments and any program changes identified during the program review process.

However, regardless of the BOP's emphasis on release preparation and planning, the inmate may choose not to participate in the offered programs, unless the program is a work assignment, mandated by federal statute, court order, or BOP policy. Programs mandated by federal statute are the literacy program for inmates who do not have a verified GED credential or high school diploma and the ESL program. Further, federal statute requires that 100 percent of eligible inmates participate in drug treatment programs.

During our audit, we found that at the institutions we visited release planning was continuous from initial classification through final release as documented in inmate files. Additionally, our review of the inmate program review reports included in the inmate files indicated that the BOP staff strongly encouraged participation in its reentry programs.

Inmate Skills Development Re-engineering Initiative

In May 2000, the BOP established an Inmate Skills Development Re-engineering Workgroup to examine how the BOP could improve efforts to equip inmates with the necessary skills to succeed upon release. The purpose of the re-engineering workgroup was to conduct an investigation of successful agencies, institutions, and programs, as well as, literature and other research, to identify best practices related to preparation of inmates for release into the community. The workgroup also utilized focus groups throughout the BOP to assist in the identification of the necessary inmate skills including, educational, vocational, interpersonal, leisure time, cognitive, wellness, and mental health.

Based on the recommendation of the re-engineering workgroup, in June 2003, the BOP established the Inmate Skills Development branch within the Correctional Programs Division. The mission of the Inmate Skills Development Branch is to "coordinate the [BOP's] efforts to implement inmate skill development initiatives and provide a centralized point of liaison with external agencies to equip inmates with the necessary skills to succeed upon release."

In order to achieve its mission the Inmate Skills Development branch has been charged with the (1) development of an inmate skill assessment process which includes the design of an individualized skill development plan to monitor progress; (2) coordination of program linkage to address skill needs; and (3) collaborative partnership building to assist with community transition.

To accurately evaluate inmate abilities and assess reentry needs, the BOP has developed an Inmate Skills Assessment Tool. The assessment tool was demonstrated over a six-month period at six institutions (one within each of the BOP's six regions) representing a wide range in security levels and male and female inmates. Currently, the BOP's Office of Research and Evaluation is conducting an evaluation of the assessment tool and related data.

FINDINGS AND RECOMMENDATIONS

I.   REENTRY PROGRAM COMPLETIONS

The BOP does not demonstrate that its institutions maximized the number of inmates that complete programs designed to prepare inmates for successful reentry into society. We found that the BOP does not ensure that: (1) institutions set realistic occupational and educational completion goals, (2) institutions are held accountable for meeting goals, (3) data for occupational and educational programs is reviewed to identify low performance, and (4) statistical data related to psychological programs and RPP performance is maintained and utilized.

As stated previously in this report, the research we reviewed related to inmate recidivism concludes that the completion of occupational, educational, psychological, and other programs during incarceration leads to a reduction in recidivism and an increase in post-release employment opportunities. We reviewed the types of programs offered by the BOP and found that the 82 institutions included in our audit offer a full range of occupational, educational, psychological, and other programs. We compared the programs offered by the BOP to the research and concluded that the BOP offers the types of programs that have been shown in these studies to better prepare inmates for successful reentry into society. Therefore, our audit focused on whether the BOP ensures that each of its institutions maximize the number inmates that successfully complete its reentry programs.

To determine the process by which the BOP monitors its reentry programs, we conducted site visits at institutions of each security level, three regional offices, and the BOP Central Office. At the institutions, we reviewed inmate files to determine whether the unit teams assessed inmate reentry program needs and monitored inmate participation in reentry programs. We found that at the institutions we visited, release planning was continuous from initial classification through final release as documented in inmate files. Additionally, our review of the inmate files revealed that the BOP staff strongly encouraged participation in its reentry programs. At the BOP Central Office and regional offices, we identified the process by which the BOP monitors reentry program performance at its institutions. We found that the BOP relies on its program review process and staff assistance visits conducted by regional office officials to monitor reentry program performance. We reviewed program review reports and staff assistance reports prepared by the BOP and found that the reports generally focused on compliance with BOP policies rather than actual program performance.

The BOP has a process that requires each institution to establish annual program completion goals. If this process is used effectively, it could ensure that each of its institutions maximize the number of inmates that participate in and complete occupational and educational programs. Each fiscal year the institution's Supervisor of Education is required to report on achievements towards the occupational and educational program goals in an Annual Program Report for Education and Recreation Services. The BOP does not require its institutions to establish goals and outcomes for psychological programs or the RPP.

According to BOP officials, since 1998 the BOP's Education Branch has systematically been working on establishing an effective strategic management process for monitoring and evaluating education program outcomes. This included the development of draft outcome based program review guidelines, that were recently issued in December 2003; directing regional staff to negotiate education completion goals for FY 2003 with the institutions; and the development of a Quarterly Performance Indicator Report to provide detailed educational program data to the institutions for verification which became operational in February 2002.

For each of the 82 institutions included in our audit, we reviewed the institution's Annual Program Report for Education and Recreation Services for FY 1999 through FY 2002 to determine whether the institutions met their occupational and educational program completion goals. We analyzed the annual reported completion goals and the institution's outcomes for occupational, GED, ESL, ACE, and parenting programs to determine whether stated goals were achieved and, as a result, whether the BOP as a whole was able to maximize the number of inmates who completed these reentry programs. For FY 2002, we also reviewed the BOP's goals and outcomes for the overall percentage of inmates enrolled in one or more educational programs during the year.

We also compared the number of inmates who completed occupational and educational programs to the number of inmates who eventually withdrew from the programs. We calculated a program performance factor, based on the number of completions divided by the number of completions plus total withdrawals for each fiscal year. (We used completion and withdrawal data that was reported in the BOP's Key Indicators system for educational and occupational programs to calculate the performance factor.)

In our judgment, this comparison is an important indicator of an institution's success and can be used to compare program performance among institutions. We were unable to analyze the percentage of inmates who completed the BOP's psychological programs and the RPP because the BOP does not maintain completion and withdrawal statistics for these programs in its Key Indicators system. The results of our performance factor calculations and comparison are described later in this report.

Institution's Annual Goals and Outcomes

As stated previously, the BOP stated that it has been working to establish an effective strategic management process for monitoring and evaluating occupational and educational goals and outcomes since 1998. However, we found that the BOP has not implemented a standardized process followed by all institutions to establish occupational and educational completion goals. Our review of the goals and outcomes reported in each institution's Annual Program Report for Education and Recreation Services for FY 1999 through FY 2002 revealed that the institutions did not always set realistic occupational, GED, ACE, and parenting goals. The institutions, in conjunction with the BOP regional offices, establish their own completion goals. Our review revealed that the goal setting process is inadequate and inconsistent, resulting in institutions setting their goals too high or too low when compared to the prior year's performance. We found instances where institutions consistently exceeded their goals for each fiscal year by a significant margin, yet failed to establish goals for the following fiscal that adequately reflected prior years outcomes.

- One institution with an occupational completion goal of 35 inmates and an actual outcome of 103 inmates completing the program in FY 2001, decreased its occupational completion goal to 20 inmates in FY 2002, but had an actual outcome of 111 inmates completing the program.

- One institution with an ESL completion goal of 60 inmates and an actual outcome of 74 inmates completing the program in FY 2001, kept the same ESL completion goal of 60 inmates in FY 2002, and had an actual outcome of 72 inmates completing the program. The same ESL completion goal of 60 inmates was also established for FY 2003.

- One institution with an ACE completion goal of 65 inmates and an actual outcome of 192 inmates completing the program in FY 2001, only increased its ACE completion goal to 120 inmates in FY 2002, and had an actual outcome of 293 inmates completing the program.

Conversely, we found institutions consistently did not meet their goals by a significant margin, yet failed to establish goals for the following fiscal that reflected prior years outcomes. For example, we found the following instances where the established goals appear inconsistent with the prior year's performance and the annual report did not include an adequate explanation for the increase or decrease in the goals from the prior year.

- One institution with a GED completion goal of 150 inmates had an actual outcome of 98 inmates completing the program in FY 1999, but increased its GED completion goal to 240 inmates in FY 2000, and had an actual outcome of 161 inmates completing the program.

- One institution with an ACE completion goal of 88 inmates had an actual outcome of 49 inmates completing the program in FY 2000, but increased its FY 2001 ACE goal to 132 completions.

Additionally, we found a lack of consistency in setting goals between institutions with similar security levels and populations. These institutions had set very different goals for the fiscal year. Further, we found that the program completion goals are stated as the number of completions rather than a percentage of completions, which does not take into account the number of enrollments or the effect the inmate population could have when comparing among institutions.

During our audit, BOP officials we interviewed agreed that the BOP should standardize the goal setting process among institutions to enhance consistency based on security level and population. In our judgment, the factors considered in setting program goals should include not only the security level of the institution and the inmate population, but also other factors such as classroom size, number of classes, number of instructors, whether the institution has a wait list for its program, and historical program completion data.

Although our audit concluded that the BOP's goal setting process is inadequate and inconsistent, we found that the completion goals were the only available source of data within the BOP we could use to determine whether the BOP institutions maximize the number of inmates that complete occupational and educational reentry programs. Therefore, we analyzed the goals and outcomes reported for each institutions' occupational, GED, ESL, ACE, and parenting programs using this information. For FY 2002, we were able to also use the National Strategic Plan goal and outcome for the percentage of inmates enrolled in one or more educational programs during the fiscal year at each institution, which was only included in the annual report for FY 2002. The details of our analysis of each institution's completion goals and outcomes for FY 2001 and FY 2002 are included in Appendix IV for occupational programs, Appendix V for GED programs (FY 2001 only), Appendix VI for ESL programs, Appendix VII for ACE programs, and Appendix VIII for parenting programs.

Overall, based on the BOP's reported information, we found that during FY 1999 through FY 2002, a large percentage of the 82 institutions included in our audit failed to meet their annual completion goals established in the Annual Program Report for Education and Recreation Services for occupational, GED, ESL, ACE, and parenting programs, as shown in the following chart.

Percentage of Institutions Failing to Meet Completions Goals by Program FY 1999 through FY 2002

	Occupational	GED	ESL	ACE	Parenting
1999	38%	49%	55%	38%	34%
2000	42%	51%	58%	31%	53%
2001	51%	39%	66%	47%	49%
2002	64%	N/A[40]	69%	45%	47%

We also found that 46 percent of the institutions we looked at failed to meet their stated National Strategic Plan goal for the percentage of inmates enrolled in one or more education programs in FY 2002 (Appendix IX).

To determine which factors may have contributed to the large percentages of institutions not meeting their occupational and educational goals, we sent questionnaires to 24 of the 82 institutions included in our audit. We selected our sample based on institution security level and inmate population as of the end of FY 2002. For each of the four security levels (minimum, low, medium, and high), we selected six institutions consisting of the two institutions with the largest inmate populations, the two institutions with the lowest inmate populations, and the two institutions with inmate populations in the middle range. We received a response to our questionnaire from all 24 institutions included in our sample. Based on the

---

[40] The BOP did not require its institutions to establish goals for its GED programs for FY 2002 because of a change in the GED testing format that was implemented at the beginning of calendar year 2002.

responses to our questions, we found that institutions that met their completion goals cited the following factors:

- The education department at the institution was fully staffed or received increased staffing during the years that the goals were met or exceeded.

- The institution added additional classes to meet its goals.

- The inmate population at the institution increased resulting in increased enrollments.

- The institution increased enrollments by shortening weekly class time allowing more inmates to be enrolled or increased class size.

- Institution staff encouraged inmates not to withdraw from the reentry programs.

- Institution staff screened inmates prior to enrollment in voluntary programs to ensure that they have the ability and are willing to commit to completing the courses.

- The unit team assisted in providing inmates with information about the program benefits and encouraged participation.

Based on the responses to our questions, we found that institutions that did not meet their completion goals cited the following factors:

- The education department was not fully staffed.

- The Supervisor of Education did not receive GED testing authorization for a significant period of time; as a result, no testing was performed during the period.

- The institution experienced a decrease in the inmate population or the number of inmates with GED needs.

- The institution's GED testing license was suspended because of a GED testing security breach.

- The institution experienced prolonged periods of lock-down.

- The institution reduced in the number of classes offered.

- Inmates did not complete the course because the course was too long.

- Inmates were transferred prior to completing the program.

Overall, we noted from the responses that institutions that met their goals appear to promote a proactive management approach (i.e., strongly encouraging inmate participation, screening applicants, and unit team involvement) and effectively used their available resources (i.e., shortening class time and adding more classes). Those institutions that did not meet their goals attributed their failure to inadequate staffing, an insufficient number of classes offered, and factors outside the control of staff such as inmate population, inmate transfers, and prolonged periods of lock-down. However, in our judgment some of these adverse factors could have been recognized and mitigated if, as noted below, the BOP had a process in place to determine why goals were not met and timely action taken to remedy poor performance.

We conducted interviews with BOP officials related to the large percentage of institutions that failed to meet their annual occupational and educational goals during FY 1999 through FY 2002. BOP officials stated that currently institutions are not held accountable for failing to meet their goals. BOP officials also stated the Central office has been moving towards performance monitoring since 1998. Currently the institutions are only held accountable for the program review guidelines, which focus on compliance with BOP policy rather than performance.

Despite the fact that the BOP's annual report process was in place and a large number of institutions failed to meet one or more of their annual occupational or educational goals during FY 1999 through FY 2002, the BOP did not have a mechanism to assess the information included in the required reports, hold institutions accountable, or redirect resources to meet emerging deficiencies. Institutions were not required to develop or implement corrective action plans to remedy performance and ensure that their goals are met in the future. In our judgment, the BOP's failure to hold institutions accountable for low performance contributed to its institutions not meeting their completion goals.

During our audit, the BOP issued a draft program review guideline that includes a review of the institution's performance towards meeting its occupational, GED, and percent participation program goals. We noted that the BOP's program reviews generally only occur every 3 years for institutions that receive a superior or good program review rating, every 2 years for institutions that receive an acceptable rating, and every

18 months for institutions that receive a deficient rating. As a result, it could be up to 3 years before corrective actions are taken for institutions that failed to meet their annual occupational and educational program goals. Further, the draft program review guidelines do not include a review of the ESL, ACE, or parenting program goals. In our judgment, the draft program review guidelines are not sufficient to ensure that corrective actions are implemented timely. We recommend that the BOP establish and implement an annual process to ensure that institutions are held accountable for meeting their occupational and educational goals and that corrective action plans are developed to remedy program performance and ensure that goals are met in future fiscal years.

We also noted during our audit that the FY 2001 Annual Program Report for Education and Recreation Services only includes the occupational and educational outcomes reported for FY 2000 and FY 2001, and the projected outcomes for FY 2002. The FY 2001 report does not include the FY 2001 occupational and educational goals for comparison with the outcomes. The FY 2001 goals can only be found in the FY 2000 Annual Program Report for Education and Recreation Services. Similarly, the FY 2002 Annual Program Report for Education and Recreation Services does not include the FY 2002 occupational and educational goals for comparison with the outcomes. We recommend that the Annual Program Report for Education and Recreation Services be revised to include both the goals and outcomes for the reported fiscal year, so that the BOP can readily determine whether its institutions meet their completion goals.

Percentage of Reentry Program Completions

In addition to reviewing each institution's occupational and educational goals and outcomes, we also compared the number of inmates who completed occupational and educational programs to the number of inmates who eventually withdrew from the programs. We calculated a program performance factor based on the number of completions divided by the number of completions plus total withdrawals for each fiscal year.[41] In our judgment, this comparison is an important indicator of an institution's success and can be used to compare program performance among institutions.

---

[41] We used completion and withdrawal data that was reported in the BOP's Key Indicators system for educational and occupational programs to calculate the performance factor.

According to BOP officials, the security level of an institution is one of the factors that can have an impact on occupational and educational program performance. For example, BOP officials stated that inmates at high security institutions are more likely to refuse programs because they are generally serving longer sentences than inmates at minimum, low, and medium security institutions. As a result, we also analyzed the performance factor by security level and determined the range in performance among the institutions within the same security level.

The BOP offers two types of occupational programs – occupational technical programs and occupational vocational programs (which includes apprenticeship programs). We calculated the performance factor for both the occupational technical and vocational programs during FY 1999 through FY 2002, based on completion and withdrawal data reported in the BOP's Key Indicators system for each of the institutions included in our audit. The details of our calculations and analysis of each institution's performance factors for FY 2001 and FY 2002 are included in Appendix IX for occupational technical programs and Appendix X for occupational vocational programs.

Based on the occupational technical and vocational performance factors, we found that during FY 1999 through FY 2002 there was a significant range in the percentage of inmates that completed occupational technical and vocational programs for each security level, as shown below.

Range in Performance Factors
Among Minimum Security Institutions
FY 1999 through FY 2002

FY	Occupational Technical		Occupational Vocational	
	Institutions Reporting	Performance Factor Range	Institutions Reporting	Performance Factor Range
1999	2	100%	10	0% - 100%
2000	1	100%	10	25% - 100%
2001	1	100%	11	50% - 100%
2002	6	75% - 100%	11	0% - 98%

Source: The OIG analysis of the completions and withdrawals for occupational technical and occupational vocational programs reported for each minimum security institution in the BOP's Key Indicators system.

Range in Performance Factors
Among Low Security Institutions
FY 1999 through FY 2002

	Occupational Technical		Occupational Vocational	
FY	Institutions Reporting	Performance Factor Range	Institutions Reporting	Performance Factor Range
1999	13	0% - 100%	20	8% - 98%
2000	15	0% - 98%	22	0% - 100%
2001	15	0% - 100%	24	0% - 100%
2002	18	6% - 100%	24	0% - 100%

Source: The OIG analysis of the completions and withdrawals for occupational technical and occupational vocational programs reported for each low security institution in the BOP's Key Indicators system.

Range in Performance Factors
Among Medium Security Institutions
FY 1999 through FY 2002

	Occupational Technical		Occupational Vocational	
FY	Institutions Reporting	Performance Factor Range	Institutions Reporting	Performance Factor Range
1999	13	0% - 100%	30	0% - 100%
2000	13	0% - 99%	30	17% - 100%
2001	12	55% - 100%	32	0% - 100%
2002	23	0% - 100%	31	25% - 100%

Source: The OIG analysis of the completions and withdrawals for occupational technical and occupational vocational programs reported for each medium security institution in the BOP's Key Indicators system.

Range in Performance Factors
Among High Security Institutions
FY 1999 through FY 2002

FY	Occupational Technical		Occupational Vocational	
	Institutions Reporting	Performance Factor Range	Institutions Reporting	Performance Factor Range
1999	2	79% - 97%	9	0% - 100%
2000	3	75% - 99%	8	0% - 100%
2001	5	0% - 100%	9	0% - 97%
2002	9	0% - 100%	11	0% - 98%

Source: The OIG analysis of the completions and withdrawals for occupational technical and occupational vocational programs reported for each high security institution in the BOP's Key Indicators system.

As shown in the previous tables, there are significant ranges in the performance factors among institutions of the same security level. The following charts further demonstrate the wide range in performance factors among institutions of the same security level for FY 2002.

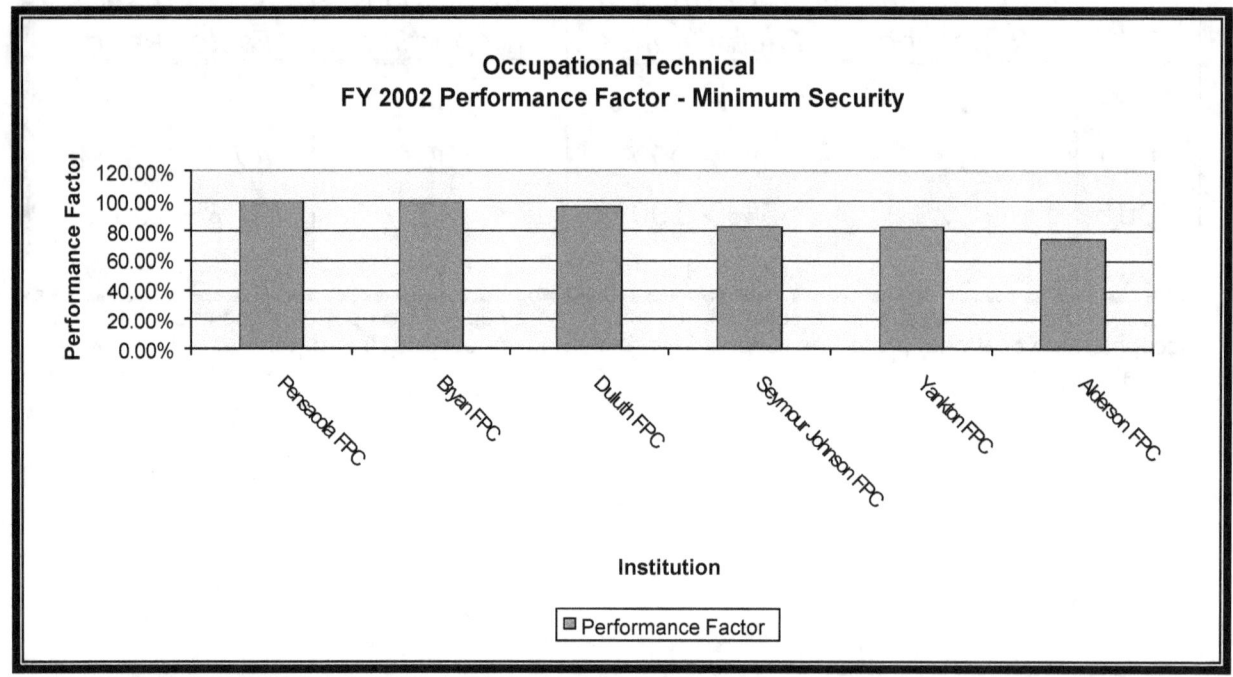

Source: The OIG analysis of the FY 2002 performance factor for occupational technical programs reported for each minimum security institution in the BOP's Key Indicators system.

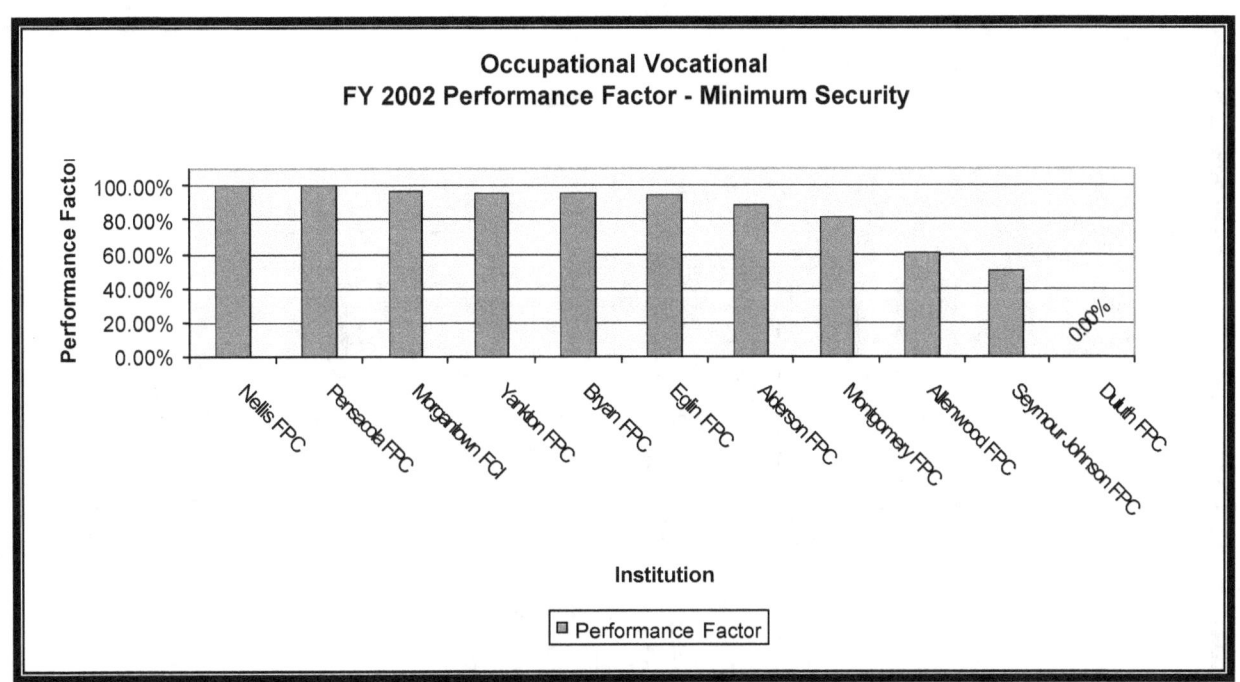

Source: The OIG analysis of the FY 2002 performance factor for occupational vocational programs reported for each minimum security institution in the BOP's Key Indicators system.

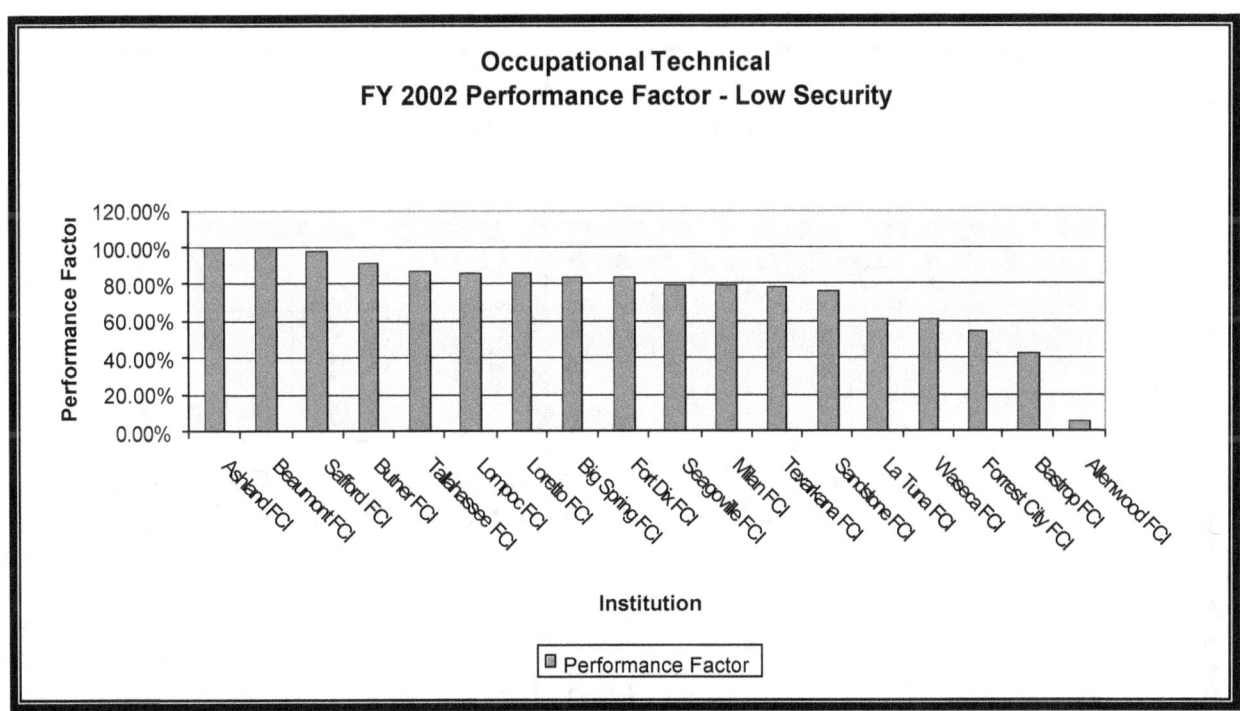

Source: The OIG analysis of the FY 2002 performance factor for occupational technical programs reported for each low security institution in the BOP's Key Indicators system.

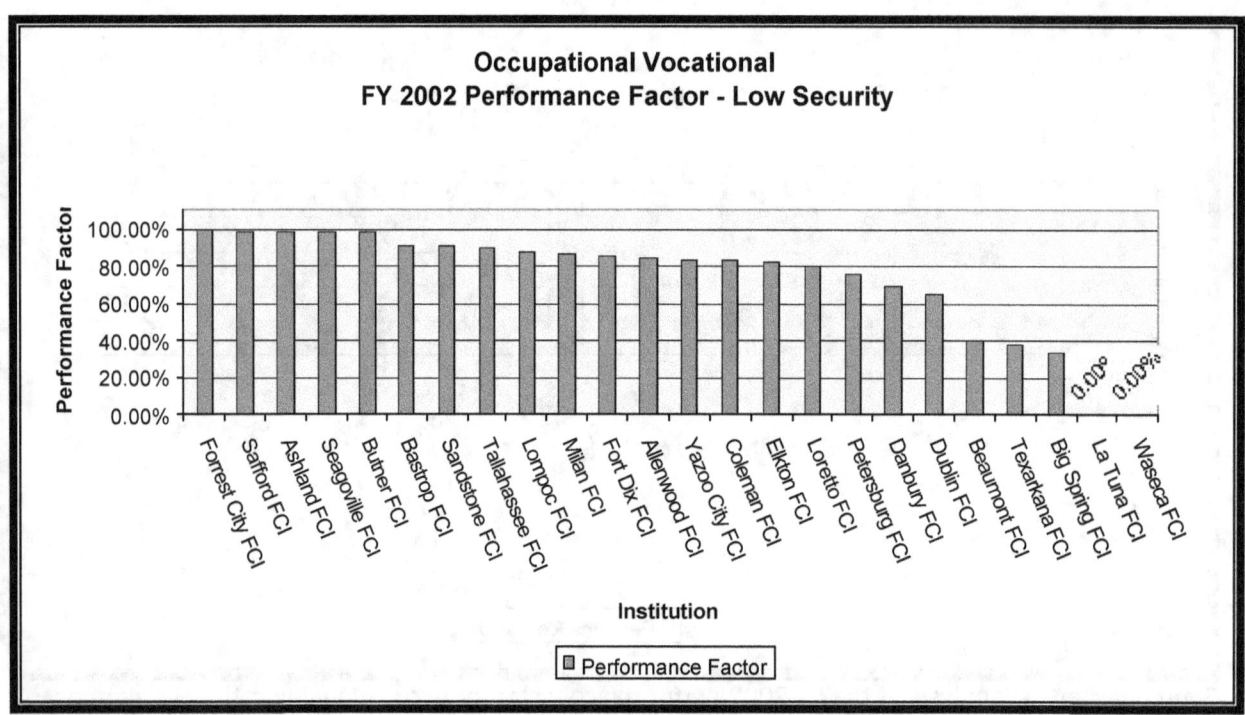

Source: The OIG analysis of the FY 2002 performance factor for occupational vocational programs reported for each low security institution in the BOP's Key Indicators system.

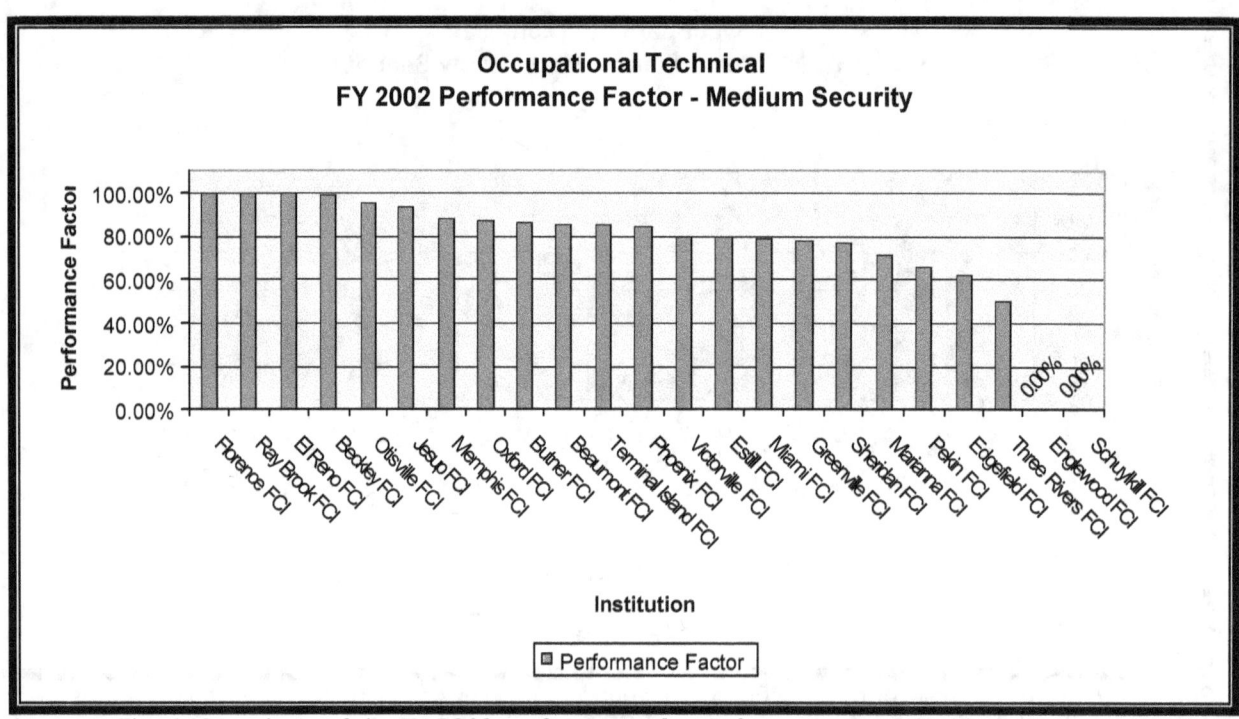

Source: The OIG analysis of the FY 2002 performance factor for occupational technical programs reported for each medium security institution in the BOP's Key Indicators system.

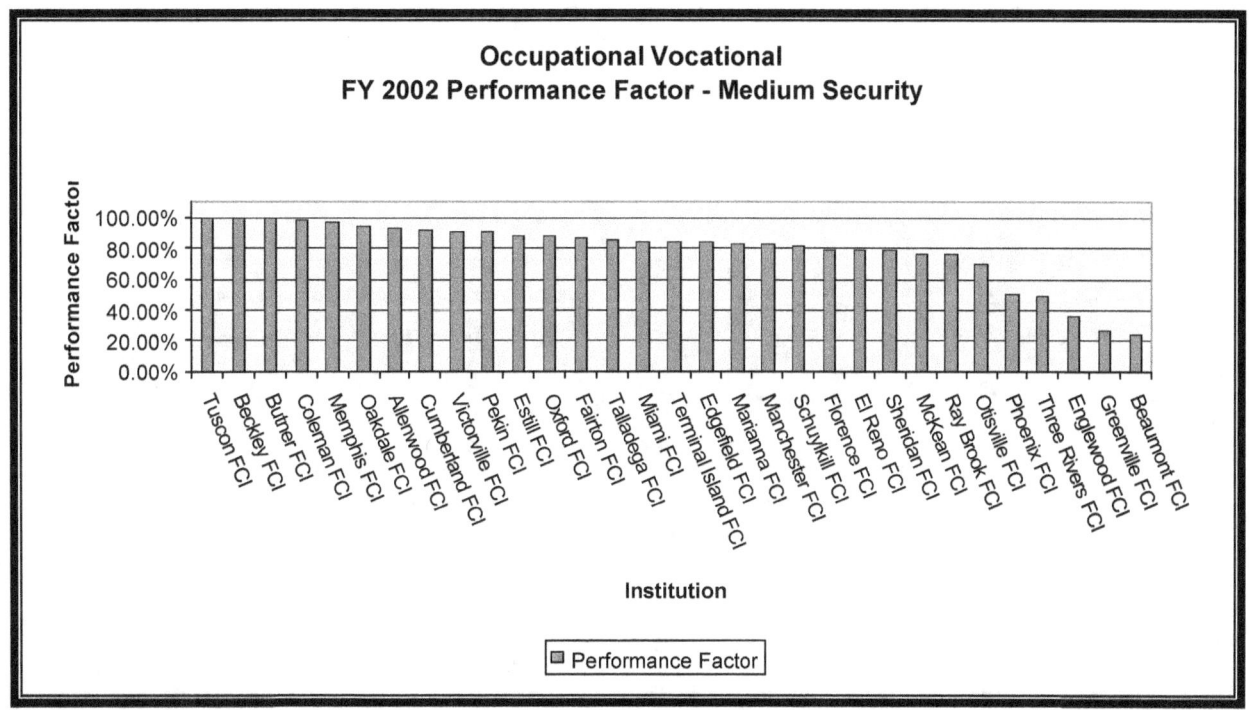

Source: The OIG analysis of the FY 2002 performance factor for occupational vocational programs reported for each medium security institution in the BOP's Key Indicators system.

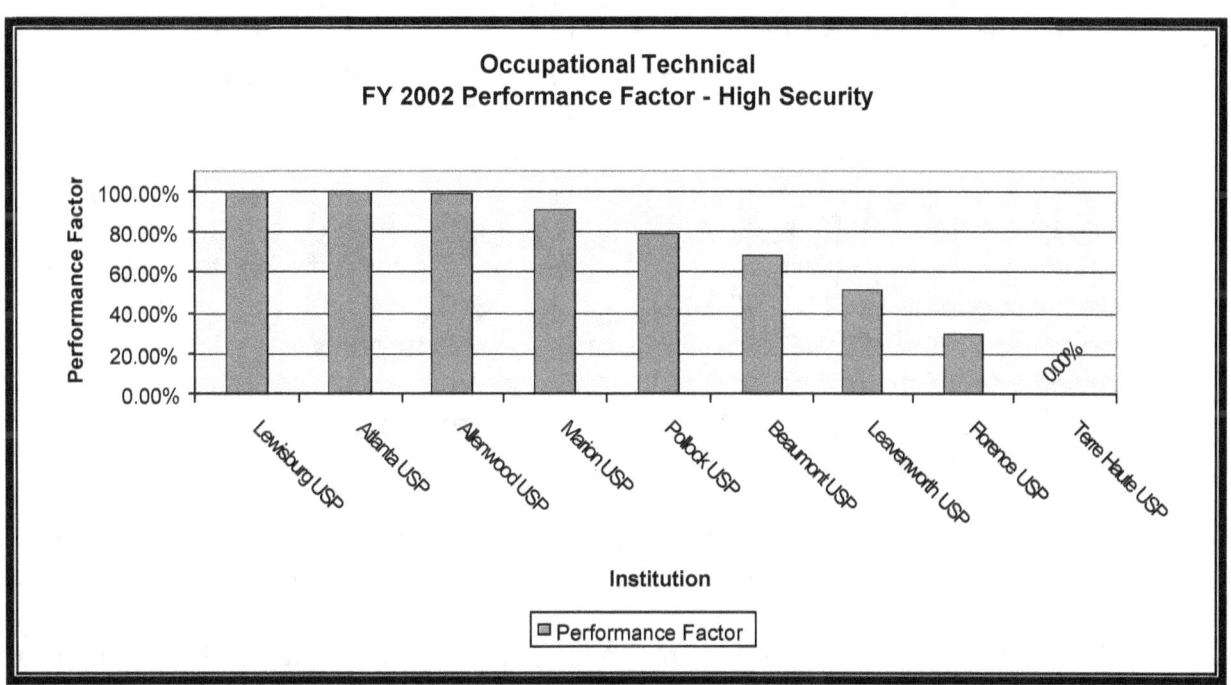

Source: The OIG analysis of the FY 2002 performance factor for occupational technical programs reported for each high security institution in the BOP's Key Indicators system.

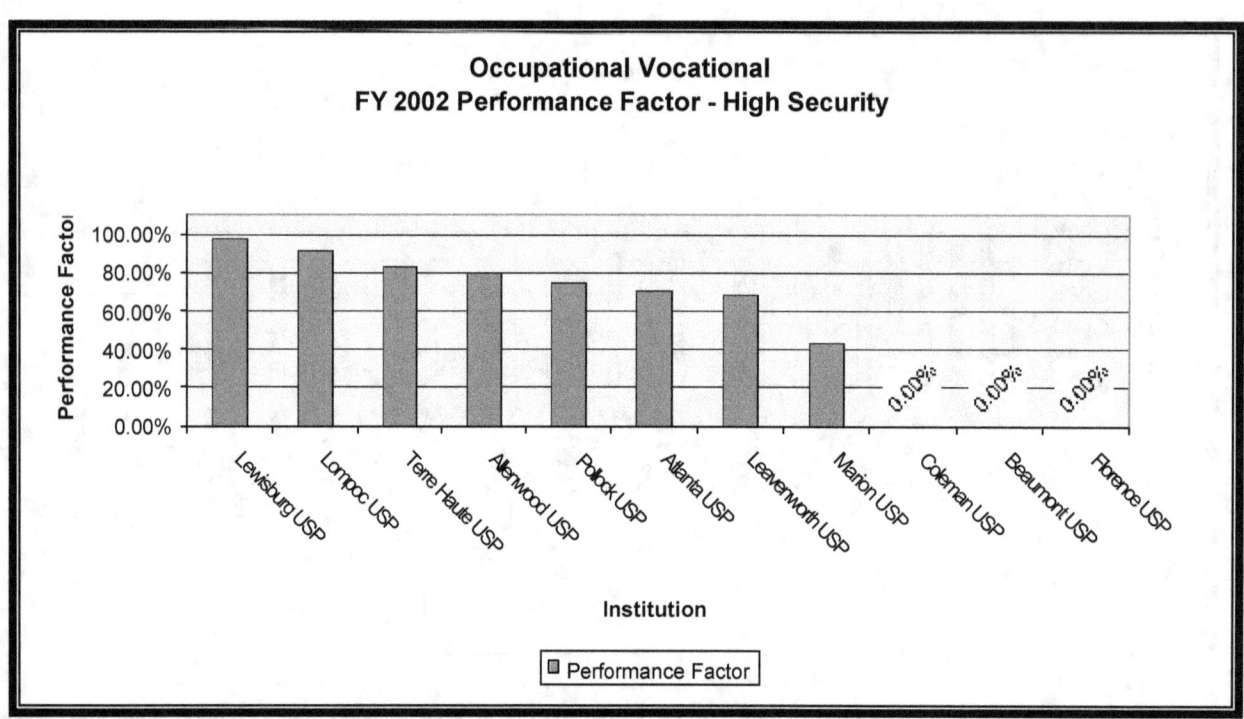

Occupational Vocational
FY 2002 Performance Factor - High Security

Source: The OIG analysis of the FY 2002 performance factor for occupational vocational programs reported for each high security institution in the BOP's Key Indicators system.

Despite the wide range in the percentage of inmates that completed occupational technical and vocational programs at institutions of the same security level, we found that similar to the occupational and educational completion goals and outcomes the BOP did not have a formal process for reviewing performance data at each institution to identify low performance.

To determine the factors that may have contributed to institutions with a low, average, or high performance factor for its occupational technical and vocational programs for FY 1999 through FY 2001, we included in our questionnaires to 24 of the 82 institutions questions pertaining to the performance factors. Based on the questionnaires, we found that institutions that had a high performance factor for occupational technical and vocational programs most commonly cited the following factors:

- Screening of inmates prior to enrollment to ensure that they have the ability and are willing to commit to completing the course.

- Support from the unit team to ensure that inmates are not transferred prior to completing the course.

- Shortening weekly class time to allow more inmates to complete the program.

- Expanding the occupational program.

- Offering programs based on inmate interests.

Based on the responses to our questions, we found that institutions that had a low performance factor for occupational technical and occupational vocational programs most commonly cited the following factors:

- Occupational programs were not fully staffed.

- Programs were eliminated because of contract or security reasons.

- Inmates were released or transferred prior to completing the program.

- Inmates withdrew from the program in order to maintain work assignments.

- Curriculum was too difficult or too long for inmates to complete.

Similar to the responses we received related to goals and outcomes, institutions with high performance rates appear to be proactive in the management and use of available resources (i.e., inmate screening, sufficient number of classes offered to meet inmate needs, and strongly encouraging inmate participation). Those institutions that did not meet their goals attribute their failure to inadequate staffing, difficult classes, and factors outside the control of staff such as inmate transfers and security issues.

We also reviewed the GED performance factor as reported in the BOP's Key Indicators system. Similar to the other areas we reviewed, we found a wide range in the percentage of inmates that completed the GED program among the BOP institutions. For example, during FY 2002

- the GED performance factor for minimum security institutions ranged from 22 to 57 percent,

- the GED performance factor for low security institutions ranged from 8 to 45 percent,

- the GED performance factor for medium security institutions ranged from 0 to 45 percent, and

- the GED performance factor for high security institutions ranged from 7 to 53 percent.

Our discussions with BOP officials during the audit revealed that they did not believe that the GED performance factor included in the BOP's Key Indicators system was an accurate assessment of its institutions' literacy programs. BOP officials felt that since the GED literacy program was a mandatory program, looking at a GED performance factor based on voluntary withdrawals would be a better measure of performance since involuntary withdrawals are often outside the control of the education department, _i.e._ the inmate might have been released or transferred prior to completing the program.

To account for the BOP's concerns, we recalculated the GED performance factor based only on voluntary withdrawals for each of the institutions included in our audit.[42] The results of our calculation revealed higher completion rates for each institution; however, we continued to find that wide ranges among institutions in the percentage of inmates that completed the GED program. For example, during FY 2002

- the GED performance factor based on voluntary withdrawals for minimum security institutions now ranged from 63 to 99 percent (compared to the 22 to 57 percent reported),

- the GED performance factor based on voluntary withdrawals for low security institutions now ranged from 49 to 97 percent (compared to the 8 to 45 percent reported),

- the GED performance factor based on voluntary withdrawals for medium security institutions now ranged from 0 to 79 percent (compared to the 0 to 45 percent reported), and

- the GED performance factor based on voluntary withdrawals for high security institutions ranged from 17 to 82 percent (compared to the 7 to 53 percent reported).

When we presented this analysis to the BOP education officials, they stated that they also did not believe that a GED performance factor based on voluntary withdrawals provided an accurate assessment of the literacy

---

[42] The GED performance factor based on voluntary withdrawals was calculated based on completions divided by completions plus voluntary withdrawals for the fiscal year.

program performance at its institutions. They felt that factors such as inmates dropping one literacy class and subsequently enrolling in a different class could increase the number of voluntary withdrawals and negatively impact the GED performance factor based on voluntary withdrawals. However, we were unable to obtain any data from the BOP that supports that the wide range in performance is solely a result of factors such as inmates dropping one literacy class and subsequently enrolling in a different class.

In our judgment, the BOP needs to develop a suitable measure of literacy program performance at its institutions. If BOP officials believe that the GED performance factor included in its Key Indicators system does not accurately measure literary program performance then it should be changed. The new performance measure should provide an accurate picture of the percentage of all inmates that arrive at the BOP institutions without a GED credential or high school diploma that complete the literacy program during incarceration.

In the absence of reliable information to measure GED program performance, we asked BOP officials how they monitor the GED program performance at the institutions. They stated that closely track the percentage of citizen inmates required to participate in the literacy program that have dropped out and are therefore not promotable above the maintenance pay grade for BOP work programs. These inmates are designated as GED Dropped Non-promotable (GED DN) in the BOP's SENTRY system.[43] The BOP's Key Indicators system also includes data on the number and percentage of GED Dropped Non-promotable inmates at each institution as of the end of the fiscal year.[44]

In our judgment, the percentage of GED Dropped Non-promotable inmates based on the BOP's SENTRY system also is not an accurate measure of literacy program performance. The percentage of GED Dropped Non-promotable inmates does not provide an accurate picture of the total number of inmates that arrive at the institution without a GED credential or high school diploma who subsequently complete the literacy program during incarceration. Further, the percentage is based on the total institution population that includes inmates who arrive at the institution with a GED

---

[43] SENTRY is the BOP's national on-line automated information system used to provide operational and management information requirements.

[44] The BOP's Key Indicators, *Current Educational Needs Fact Sheet*.

credential or high school diploma and inmates whose GED status is unknown.

Nonetheless, since BOP officials indicated that they closely track the percentage of GED Dropped Non-promotable inmates, and this information is included in the BOP's Key Indicators system, we also reviewed these percentages for each security level and each institution included in our audit for FY 1999 through FY 2002. The details of our review of the percentage of GED Dropped Non-promotable inmates at each institution for FY 2001 and FY 2002 are included in Appendix XI. We found that for each security level the percentage of GED Dropped Non-promotable inmates generally decreased from FY 1999 through FY 2002. However, as with the other areas we looked at, we found a significant range among institutions at the same security level. Specifically,

- For FY 1999, there was an 88 percent difference in the percentage of GED Dropped Non-promotable inmates between the lowest and highest minimum security institutions, a 90 percent difference between the low security institutions, a 96 percent difference between the medium security institutions, and a 60 percent difference between the high security institutions.

- For FY 2000, there was a 90 percent difference in the percentage of GED Dropped Non-promotable inmates between the lowest and highest minimum security institutions, an 85 percent difference between the low security institutions, a 94 percent difference between the medium security institutions, and a 72 percent difference between the high security institutions.

- For FY 2001, there was a 93 percent difference in the percentage of GED Dropped Non-promotable inmates between the lowest and highest minimum security institutions, a 93 percent difference between the low security institutions, a 91 percent difference between the medium security institutions, and a 60 percent difference between the high security institutions.

- For FY 2002, there was a 96 percent difference in the percentage of GED Dropped Non-promotable inmates between the lowest and highest minimum security institutions, a 93 percent difference between the low security institutions, a 93 percent difference between the medium security institutions, and a 59 percent difference between the high security institutions.

We also noted that the BOP maintains data on the percentage of noncitizen inmates required to participate in the literacy program that have dropped out and are therefore subject to a loss of good conduct time. These inmates are designated as Exempt GED Non-promotable (GED XN) in the BOP's SENTRY system. The BOP's Key Indicators system also includes data on the number and percentage of Exempt GED Non-promotable inmates at each institution as of the fiscal year-end.

We reviewed the percentage of Exempt GED Non-promotable inmates for each security level during FY 1999 through FY 2002 based on the data contained in the BOP's Key Indicators system. We found that, with the exception of minimum security institutions, for each security level as a whole the percentage of Exempt GED Non-promotable inmates increased from FY 1999 through FY 2002, as shown in the following charts.

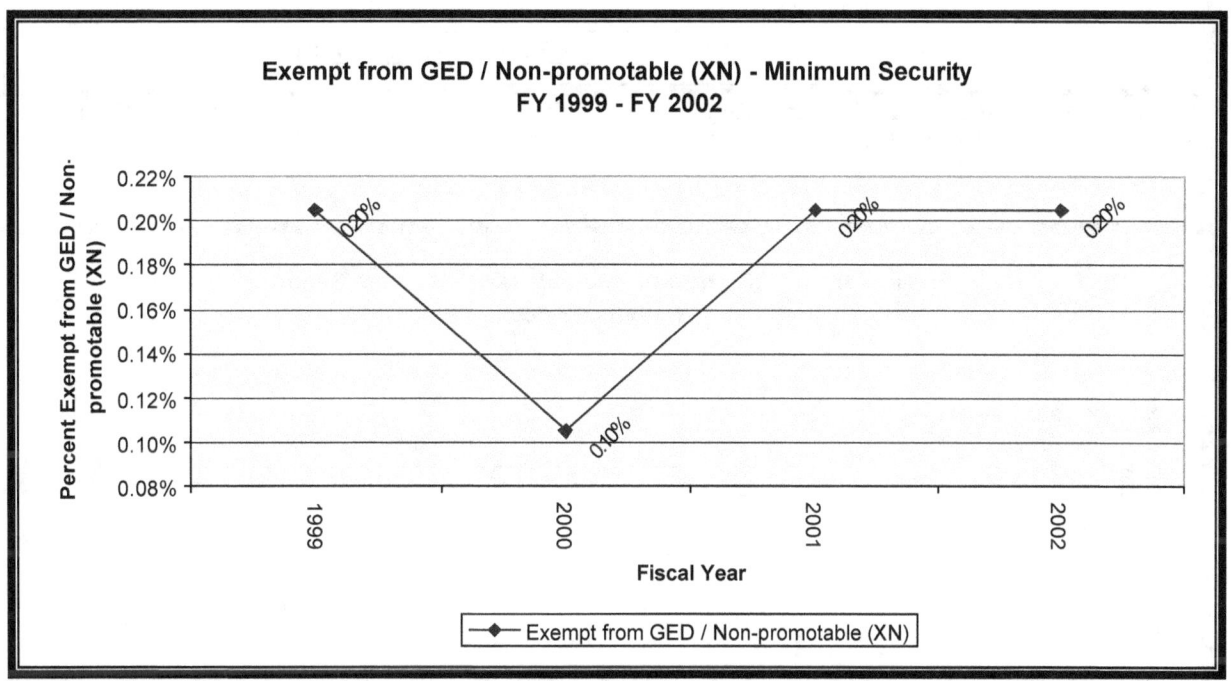

Source: The OIG analysis of the percentage Exempt GED Non-promotable inmates at minimum security institutions reported in the BOP's Key Indicators system for FY 1999 through FY 2002.

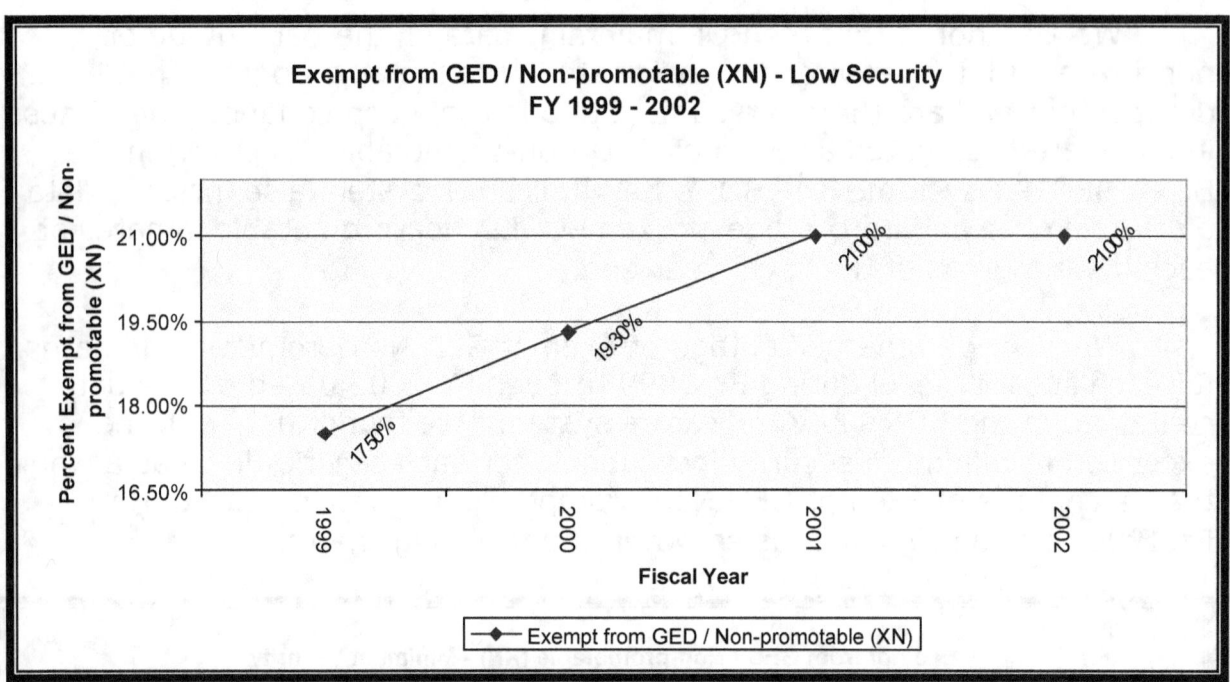

Source: The OIG analysis of the percentage Exempt GED Non-promotable inmates at low security institutions reported in the BOP's Key Indicators system for FY 1999 through FY 2002.

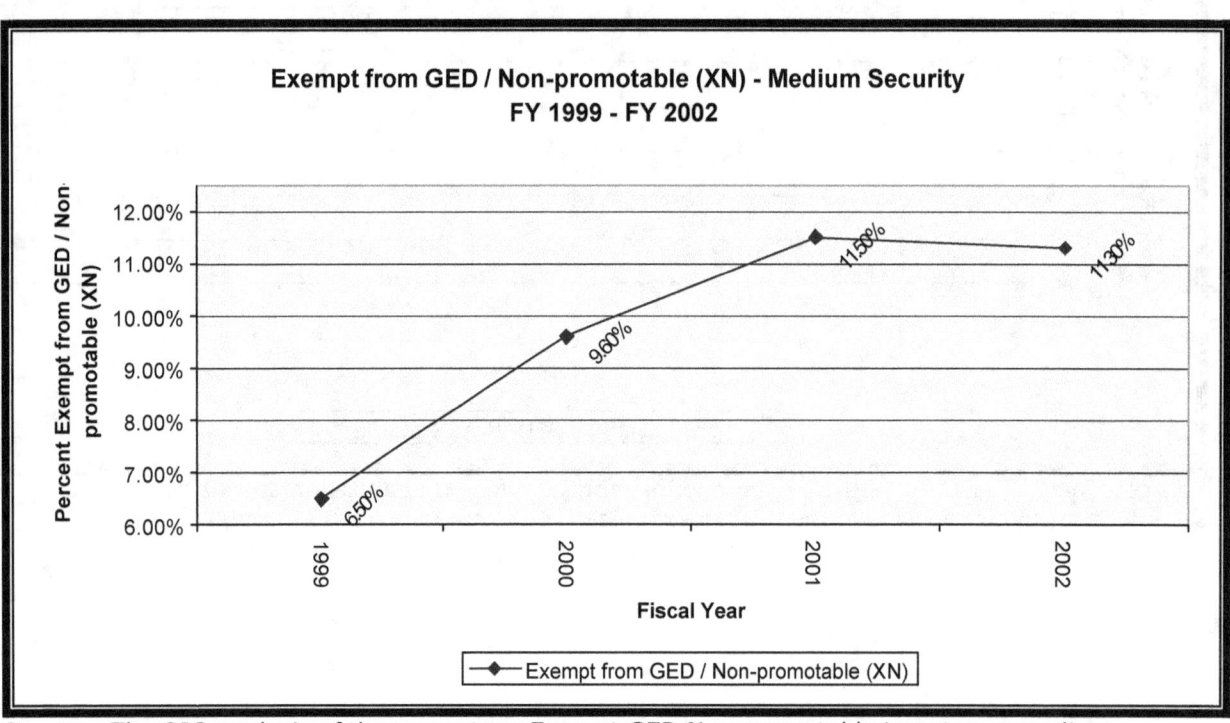

Source: The OIG analysis of the percentage Exempt GED Non-promotable inmates at medium security institutions reported in the BOP's Key Indicators system for FY 1999 through FY 2002.

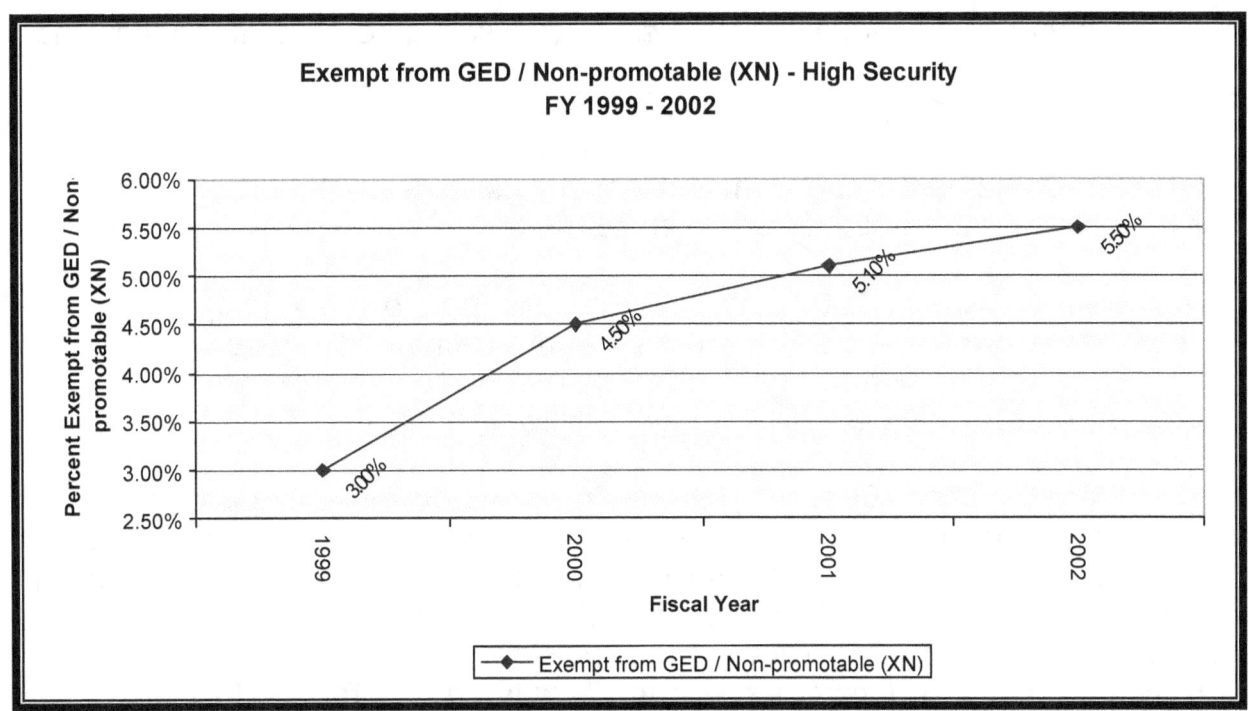

Exempt from GED / Non-promotable (XN) - High Security
FY 1999 - 2002

Source: The OIG analysis of the percentage Exempt GED Non-promotable inmates at high security institutions reported in the BOP's Key Indicators system for FY 1999 through FY 2002.

As shown in the previous charts, the percentage of Exempt GED Non-promotable inmates increased for each security level from FY 1999 through FY 2002. Therefore, in our judgment, the BOP has not adequately monitored the percentage of noncitizen inmates that have dropped out of the GED program.

Psychological Programs and RPP Participation

As stated previously, we were unable to analyze the percentage of inmates who complete the BOP's psychological programs because the BOP does not maintain completion and withdrawal statistics for these programs in its Key Indicators system.

In its budget, the BOP tracks the following performance indicators related to its psychological programs:

- percentage of inmates in residential drug treatment,

- number of inmates in non-residential drug treatment,

- percentage of intake assessments,

- number of individual therapy/crisis counseling sessions provided, and

- number of suicide risk assessments.

However, these performance indicators only cover a small portion of the psychological programs offered by the BOP.

Prior to January 2003, the BOP did not report on psychological program performance data for most of its programs. As a result, we were unable to use this data to analyze trends related to performance, such as completion rates, failure rates, and withdrawal rates.

Since January 2003, the BOP has reported on monthly participation data for the majority of its psychological programs; however, this data is still not included in its Key Indicators system. The data provided in the monthly reports prepared by the BOP's Office of Research and Evaluation includes: (1) admissions, (2) completions, (3) expulsions, (4) failures, (5) withdrawals, (6) incompletes, and (7) waiting lists for the following programs.

- Residential Drug Abuse Treatment Program,

- Non-Residential Drug Abuse Treatment Program,

- Transitional Drug Abuse Treatment Program,

- BRAVE Program,

- CODE Program,

- New Pathways Program, and

- Sex Offender Treatment Program.

BOP officials stated that the participation data is a tool but not necessarily a measure of performance. For example, BOP officials stated that a large failure or expulsion rate in a psychological program is not necessarily an indication of low performance because sometimes expulsions are necessary to hold inmates accountable for their actions.

BOP officials also stated that it is difficult to evaluate performance of psychological programs since they are dealing with human behavior that is not easily determined based on completion rates or other data and that statistical data for these types of programs is best used as a tool to evaluate trends over a period of time. In our judgment, participation data of this nature is also relevant and should be used by management as an indicator of potential immediate concerns. For example, a large number of withdrawals could indicate inmates are being transferred to another institution prior to completing a program. In addition, a large number of expulsions, failures, and withdrawals also may indicate a problem related to a specific psychological program at an institution.

At each of the three regional offices included in our audit, we identified the process for evaluating the monthly psychological program participation data for the institutions in their respective areas. We found that the BOP regional offices did not have a standardized process for evaluating the participation data or holding its institutions accountable for low participation. Generally, if the regional officials stated that if they noted trends in the participation data, such as a high failure rate in a particular program on the monthly participation report, they would follow-up by telephone. However, we found no formal review process in place at the regional level.

As with its psychological programs, we found that he BOP does not maintain completion and withdrawal statistics for the RPP in its Key Indicators system. Additionally, one of the expected outcomes of the BOP's RPP is that inmate recidivism will be reduced. Yet, the BOP has not conducted any studies demonstrating that successful participation in its RPP leads to a reduction in recidivism.

All eligible inmates committed to BOP custody are required to participate in the RPP and must enroll in the program no later than 30 months prior to release to the community or a CCC. Although the BOP can determine the RPP status of each inmate at any given point in time, no statistical data related to RPP performance is tracked.

At each of the three regional offices included in our audit, we identified the process for evaluating RPP participation for its institutions. We found that two of the three regional offices did not review RPP participation. The third, the Northeast Regional Office, sends a monthly roster to each of its institutions listing those inmates within 30 months of release that have not enrolled in the RPP. However, no formal response is required from the institutions. The BOP should, at a minimum, track participation data for its institutions to determine the percentage of eligible inmates that have completed the RPP prior to release into the community. Based on our discussions with BOP officials, we determined that the percentage of eligible inmates that have completed the RPP prior to release into the community could be included in its Key Indicators system.

In addition to tracking the percentage of eligible inmates that have completed the RPP prior to release into the community, the BOP needs to establish a mechanism to hold institutions accountable for RPP performance and implement corrective actions plans to remedy low performance.

Conclusion

In summary, we found that the BOP does not ensure that:
(1) institutions set realistic occupational and educational completion goals, (2) institutions are held accountable for meeting goals, (3) data for occupational, educational, and psychological programs is reviewed to identify low performance, and (4) statistical data related to RPP performance is not maintained. As a result, we concluded that the BOP does not provide assurance that each of its institutions maximized the number of inmates that complete programs designed to prepare inmates for successful reentry into society.

Recommendations

We recommend that the BOP:

1. Ensure that a formalized process is established to set realistic occupational and educational completion goals stated as a percentage of completions to account for total enrollments and inmate population. The factors considered in setting educational goals should include the security level of the institution, inmate population, classroom size, number of classes, number of instructors, whether the institution has a wait list for its programs, and historical educational program completion data.

2. Establish and implement a formal process to ensure that institutions are held accountable for meeting their occupational and educational goals and that corrective action plans are developed to remedy performance so that goals are met in future years.

3. Revise the Annual Program Report for Education and Recreation Services to include both the occupational and educational goals and outcomes for the reported fiscal year so that the BOP can readily determine whether the institution met its goals.

4. Establish and implement a formal standardized process for evaluating the performance factor for occupational technical and vocational programs on an annual basis to ensure that the BOP institutions are held accountable for low performance and that corrective action plans are developed to remedy occupational program performance.

5. Ensure that a formal standardized process is developed and implemented to screen all inmates prior to enrollment in all occupational programs to ensure that they have the ability and are willing to commit to completing the course.

6. Ensure that a suitable measure of literacy program performance is developed to evaluate its institutions. The new performance measure should provide an accurate picture of the percentage of all inmates that arrive at the BOP institutions without a GED credential or high school diploma who complete the literacy program during incarceration.

7. Ensure that the percentage of citizen inmates required to participate in the literacy program that have dropped out at each institution is more closely evaluated.

8. Ensure that the percentage of noncitizen inmates that have dropped out of the literacy program at each institution is monitored.

9. Establish and implement a mechanism to hold institutions accountable for the monthly psychological program participation data that includes corrective action plans for institutions with low participation.

10. Ensure that participation data is tracked for all of the BOP institutions to determine the percentage of eligible inmates that have completed the RPP prior to release into the community.

11. Establish and implement a mechanism to hold institutions accountable for RPP performance that includes corrective action plans for institutions with low performance.

II.   Community Corrections Centers (CCC)

The BOP offers transitional services to inmates through CCC placement, which has been found to increase the chances of successful reentry into society. The BOP establishes CCC utilization targets for its minimum, low, and medium security institutions. However, our audit revealed that a large number of institutions failed to meet their CCC utilization targets during FY 2000 through FY 2002. Also, the BOP has not developed a CCC utilization target for its high security institutions, and does not adequately ensure that all eligible inmates are provided the opportunity to transition through a CCC in preparation for reentry into society.

In addition to reentry programs offered to inmates while serving their sentences at BOP institutions, the BOP provides services that assist inmates when they transition from incarceration into the community. The primary transitional service provided by the BOP is the placement of inmates in CCCs, also known as halfway houses. Pursuant to 18 U.S.C. § 3624(c), the BOP is required, to the extent possible, to assure that inmates spend a reasonable part of their term of incarceration under conditions that will afford the prisoner a reasonable opportunity to adjust to and prepare for reentry into the community. The BOP believes the transitional services provided through a CCC meet the requirements of 18 U.S.C. § 3624(c). Pursuant to this federal statute, the BOP can place inmates in a CCC for a period not to exceed the last 6 months of confinement or a period equal to 10 percent of the inmate's sentence, whichever is less.

At the institutions we visited, we reviewed inmate files to determine whether eligible inmates were placed in CCCs prior to release. We found that the unit team generally referred eligible inmates for CCC placement; however, not all inmates referred for CCC placement were transitioned through a CCC. The reasons that those inmates that were not transitioned through a CCC included that the inmates (1) were not eligible (e.g., were deportable aliens), (2) were considered a flight risk, (3) were considered a high risk, or (4) refused placement.

BOP policy requires that eligible inmates be released to the community through a CCC. However, the policy also states that the BOP does not ordinarily consider the following inmates for CCC programs.[45]

- Inmates who are assigned a "Sex Offender" Public Safety Factor.

- Inmates who are assigned a "Deportable Alien" Public Safety Factor.

- Inmates who require inpatient medical, psychological, or psychiatric treatment.

- Inmates who refuse to participate in the Inmate Financial Responsibility Program.

- Inmates who refuse to participate, withdraw, are expelled, or otherwise fail to meet attendance and examination requirements in a required Drug Abuse Education program.

- Inmates serving sentences of 6 months or less.

- Inmates who refuse to participate in the RPP.

- Inmates who pose a significant threat to the community. These are inmates whose current offense or behavioral history suggests a substantial or continuing threat to the community.

BOP officials we interviewed believe that CCCs provide an excellent transitional environment for inmates nearing the end of their sentences. According to the BOP, during the transitional period at a CCC, inmate activities are closely monitored, and inmates are provided with a suitable residence, structured programs, job placement and counseling. CCCs also offer drug testing and counseling for alcohol and drug-related problems. Further, during their stay inmates are required to pay a subsistence charge to defer the cost of their confinement in a CCC (25 percent of their gross income, not to exceed the average daily cost of their CCC placement).

A strategic objective of the BOP sets target CCC utilization rates for minimum, low, and medium security institutions.[46] (The CCC utilization rate

---

[45] BOP Program Statement No. 7310.04, *Community Corrections Center (CCC) Utilization and Transfer Procedure*, dated December 16, 1998.

[46] The BOP, *State of the Bureau 2002, Accomplishments and Goals*.

is the percentage of inmates transitioned into the community through a CCC, as compared to the percentage of inmates released directly into the community.) The target CCC utilization rates are shown below.

Target CCC Utilization Rates

Security Level	CCC Utilization Target
Minimum Security	80 percent
Low Security	70 percent
Medium Security	65 percent

As stated previously, BOP policy requires that eligible inmates be released to the community through a CCC, regardless of security level.[47] Nonetheless, we noted that the BOP has not established a CCC utilization target for its high security institutions. We found that the average CCC utilization rate for the BOP high security institutions was 23 percent in FY 2000, 39 percent in FY 2001, and 45 percent in FY 2002. In its policy, the BOP also states that one reason for referring an inmate to a CCC prior to release directly into the community is to increase public safety by aiding in the transition of an inmate into the community. In our judgment, inmates in high security institutions have the greatest need for transitioning through the controlled CCC environment prior to being released directly into the community, especially since the average sentence of inmates placed in high security institutions was 12 years as of the end of FY 2002.

Historically, BOP officials at high security institutions have been reluctant to place their inmates in CCCs prior to release because they were considered a public safety risk. Nonetheless, in our judgment the BOP should also establish a CCC utilization target for its high security institutions to ensure that eligible inmates released from these institutions are provided with the same opportunity to transition through a CCC prior to release into the community. During the course of our audit, several BOP officials at the regional offices concurred that a CCC utilization target should be set for the high security institutions. In establishing a CCC utilization target for its high security institutions, the BOP should consider the average CCC utilization rates noted in the preceding paragraph.

---

[47] BOP Program Statement No. 7310.04, *Community Corrections Center (CCC) Utilization and Transfer Procedure*, dated December 16, 1998.

The 82 institutions we reviewed included 13 high security institutions and 1 maximum security institution. Therefore, we were only able to review the CCC utilization targets and outcomes during FY 2000 through FY 2002 for the remaining 68 minimum, low, and medium security institutions. We used the total number of inmates transferred to a CCC and the total number of inmates released directly to the community as reported in the BOP's Key Indicators system to calculate the CCC utilization rate for each institution and compared this calculation to the BOP's CCC utilization targets. The details of our calculations and analysis of each institution's CCC utilization rate for FY 2001 and FY 2002 are included in Appendix XII.

Overall, the results of our review revealed that a large number of institutions failed to meet the BOP's stated CCC utilization targets for FY 2000 through FY 2002. Specifically, we found the following for each fiscal year.

- For the 67 institutions reporting in FY 2000, 36 (54 percent) failed to meet their CCC utilization target for that fiscal year.

- For the 67 institutions reporting in FY 2001, 19 (28 percent) failed to meet their CCC utilization target for that fiscal year.

- For the 68 institutions reporting in FY 2002, 27 (40 percent) failed to meet their CCC utilization target for that fiscal year.

Since the BOP established its CCC utilization targets by security level, we analyzed the CCC utilization targets and outcomes by security level and determined the range in performance among the institutions within the same security level.

Our analysis of the CCC utilization targets and outcomes by security level revealed that for FY 2000, none of the 11 minimum security institutions reporting failed to meet their CCC utilization target, 14 (58 percent) of the 24 low security institutions reporting failed to meet their CCC utilization target, and 22 (69 percent) of the 32 medium security institutions reporting failed to meet their CCC utilization target.

Additionally, for each security level there was generally a significant range in the CCC utilization rates achieved by each institution (Appendix XIII), as shown in the following charts.

CCC Utilization Rates Achieved
Among Minimum Security Institutions
FY 2000 through FY 2002

FY	Institutions Reporting	CCC Utilization Rate Range
2000	11	81% - 97%
2001	11	81% - 94%
2002	11	80% - 96%

CCC Utilization Rates Achieved
Among Low Security Institutions
FY 2000 through FY 2002

FY	Institutions Reporting	CCC Utilization Rate Range
2000	24	47% - 86%
2001	24	56% - 88%
2002	24	52% - 83%

CCC Utilization Rates Achieved
Among Medium Security Institutions
FY 2000 through FY 2002

FY	Institutions Reporting	CCC Utilization Rate Range
2000	32	42% - 100%
2001	32	54% - 89%
2002	33	35% - 88%

CCC Utilization Rates Achieved Among High Security Institutions FY 2000 through FY 2002

FY	Institutions Reporting	CCC Utilization Rate Range
2000	9	0% - 36%
2001	11	0% - 56%
2002	13	0% - 75%

To determine the factors that may have contributed to institutions not meeting their CCC utilization targets during FY 2000 through FY 2002, we included questions regarding the CCC utilization rates in the questionnaires we sent to 24 institutions, as discussed in Finding I of this report. Based on the responses to our questions, we found that institutions that met their CCC utilization targets most commonly cited the following factors:

- The prior BOP Director and executive staff strongly encouraged institutions to refer inmates for CCC placement.

- Institution staff stressed the use and referral for CCC placement at unit team meetings and staff strongly encouraged inmates to participate.

- The institution started the CCC referral process early, especially in cases of inmates with short sentences.

- Eligible inmates who have completed the Residential Drug Abuse Program and qualified for the one-year sentence reduction received mandatory CCC placement.

- Institution staff counseled inmates who initially refuse CCC placement about the benefits of the program.

Based on the responses to our questionnaires, we found that institutions that did not meet their CCC utilization targets most commonly cited the following factors:

- The institution applied a conservative interpretation of the BOP's policy regarding the eligibility of inmates for CCC placement.

- The institution had a large number of inmates who declined CCC placement.

- The institution had a large number of inmates with pending charges in other districts and inmates with short sentences.

Overall, institutions that met their goals attributed their success to support from executive staff and unit teams that strongly encourage inmate participation. Those institutions that did not meet their goals attributed their failure to conservative interpretation of policy and factors outside the control of staff, such as a large percentage of inmates that were ineligible for CCC placement.

According to BOP officials, at each quarterly executive staff meeting CCC utilization rates are reviewed and the regional directors may be asked to comment on any utilization rate outliers (institutions with CCC utilization rates that are significantly lower than the target utilization rate). BOP officials also stated that the regional directors are ultimately held responsible for monitoring the CCC utilization rates within their region. Although quarterly meetings are held and regional directors monitor their respective regional progress, only one specific security level (minimum, low, medium or high) is addressed at each quarterly meeting and each regional director may have a different process for monitoring CCC utilization rates. However, as shown previously, we found that during FY 2000 through FY 2002, between 28 and 54 percent of institutions we looked at failed to meet their CCC utilization targets.

As with the other areas we reviewed, this may be attributed BOP regional offices did not follow a formal standardized process to ensure that institutions are held accountable for meeting their targets and that corrective action plans are developed to remedy low CCC utilization. At each of the three regional offices we identified the process for reviewing CCC utilization rates and found that each of the three regional offices had different processes. For example, one regional office did not have a process in place for reviewing CCC utilization rates, while another reviewed the rates but did not necessarily follow-up consistently with institutions that did not meet their targets.

Conversely, the Northeast Regional Office has established a formal process to ensure that all eligible inmates at each of its institutions are provided the opportunity to transition into the community through a CCC. The Northeast Regional Office officials review the CCC utilization data contained in Key Indicators system and the quarterly CCC utilization report

56

prepared by the BOP's Central Office in order to determine if its institutions are "on track" to meet established CCC utilization targets. Further, the Northeast Regional Office requires each of its institutions to submit a monthly CCC utilization report identifying both the number of inmates referred for and those denied CCC placement. For all inmates denied CCC placement, regional officials ask the institution to provide a detailed explanation regarding the basis for the inmate's CCC denial. Regional officials then review each denial in order to determine whether the denial is in compliance with the CCC utilization policy.

We also found that the CCC utilization rates and targets cannot be used to determine whether all eligible inmates at each institution were released to the community through a CCC, as required by BOP policy. Currently, the CCC utilization targets range from 65 percent for medium security level institutions to 80 percent for minimum security level institutions (a CCC utilization target has not been established for high security level institutions). Therefore, even if an institution achieves or exceeds the CCC utilization target for its security level, the BOP does not assure that all eligible inmates were transitioned through a CCC. In our judgment implementing a formal process for reviewing eligible inmates that are denied CCC placement, similar to the Northeast Regional Office, would also ensure that all eligible inmates are placed in a CCC prior to release.

It should be noted that subsequent to our audit, the BOP proposed a revision to the CCC utilization targets including the establishment of a CCC utilization target for high security level institutions and increasing the targets for minimum, low and medium security level institutions. However, to date the BOP has not approved or implemented the proposed revisions to the CCC utilization targets.

Recommendations

We recommend that the BOP:

12. Establish a CCC utilization target for its high security institutions.

13. Establish and implement a formal process to ensure that all eligible inmates are placed in a CCC prior to release.

STATEMENT ON COMPLIANCE WITH
LAWS AND REGULATIONS

We conducted our audit of the BOP preparation of Inmates for Reentry into Society in accordance with *Government Auditing Standards*. As required by the standards, we audited the BOP's programs designed to prepare inmates for reentry into society in order to obtain reasonable assurance that the BOP complied with laws and regulations, that, if not complied with, in our judgment could have a material effect on the administration its programs. Compliance with laws and regulations related to the preparation of inmates for reentry into society is the responsibility of the BOP management. An audit includes examining, on a test basis, evidence about compliance with laws and regulations. At the time of our audit, the pertinent legislation and the applicable regulations were the:

- Violent Crime Control and Law Enforcement Act of 1994 (VCCLEA),

- Prison Litigation Reform Act of 1995 (PLRA), and

- Crime Control Act of 1990.

Except for the issues discussed in the Findings and Recommendations section of this report, nothing came to our attention that caused us to believe that the BOP management was not in compliance with the laws listed above.

STATEMENT ON MANAGEMENT CONTROLS

In planning and performing our audit of the BOP Preparation of Inmates for Reentry into Society, we considered the BOP's management controls for the purpose of determining our auditing procedures. The evaluation was not made for the purpose of providing assurance on the management control structure as a whole; however, we noted certain matters that we consider reportable conditions under generally accepted government auditing standards.

- The BOP did not ensure that its institutions set realistic occupational and educational completion goals. Further, the program completion goals are stated as the number of completions rather than a percentage of completions, which does not accurately reflect program performance because it does not take into account the number of enrollments or the inmate population, see Finding I.

- The BOP did not have a mechanism in place to hold institutions accountable for meeting goals. Additionally, institutions were not required to develop or implement corrective actions plans to remedy performance and ensure that goals are met in the future, see Finding I.

- Despite the wide range in the percentage of inmates that successfully completed occupational programs and the percentage of inmates that withdrew from the mandatory GED program at institutions of the same security level, the BOP did not use the data for reviewing program performance at each of its institutions, see Finding I.

- The BOP has only tracked the participation data for most of its psychological programs since January 2003. However, the BOP does not use its data for reviewing program participation at each of its institutions, see Finding I.

- The BOP also does not track the percentage of inmates that successfully complete the RPP at each of its institutions prior to release, see Finding I.

- The BOP has not established a CCC utilization target for its high security institutions. Additionally, the BOP does not have a formal standardized process to ensure that institutions are held accountable for meeting their goals and that corrective actions plans are developed to remedy low CCC utilization, see Finding II.

- The CCC utilization rates and targets cannot be used to determine whether all eligible inmates at each institution were released to the community through a CCC, as required by BOP policy, see Finding II.

Because we are not expressing an opinion on the BOP's overall management control structure, this statement is intended solely for the information and use of the BOP in managing its programs designed to prepare inmates for reentry into society.

OBJECTIVES, SCOPE, AND METHODOLOGY

The purpose of our audit was to determine whether the BOP ensures that federal inmates benefit from its programs designed to prepare inmates for successful reentry into society. The objectives of our audit were to determine whether the BOP ensures that each of its institutions maximize the number inmates that complete programs designed to prepare inmates for reentry into society including occupational, educational, psychological, and other programs; and all eligible inmates are provided the opportunity to transition through a CCC in preparation for reentry into society.

We conducted our audit in accordance with *Government Auditing Standards*. We included such tests as were necessary to accomplish the audit objectives.

We conducted fieldwork at the BOP Central Office, and conducted field work and/or obtained information through questionnaires from the following BOP regional offices and institutions:

- North Central Regional Office, Kansas City, Kansas;

- Northeast Regional Office, Philadelphia, Pennsylvania;

- South Central Regional Office, Dallas, Texas;

- FPC Alderson, Alderson, West Virginia;

- USP Allenwood, White Deer, Pennsylvania;

- USP Atlanta, Atlanta, Georgia;

- FCI Bastrop, Bastrop, Texas;

- FCI Beaumont, Beaumont, Texas;

- FCI Beckley, Beaver, West Virginia;

- FCI Butner, Butner, North Carolina;

- FPC Eglin, Eglin, Florida;

- FCI El Reno, El Reno, Oklahoma;

- FCI Elkton, Elkton, Ohio;

- FCI Englewood, Englewood, Colorado;

- ADX Florence, Florence, Colorado;

- FCI Florence and the adjacent camp, Florence, Colorado;

- USP Florence, Florence, Colorado;

- FCI Fort Dix, Fort Dix, New Jersey;

- FCI Greenville, Greenville, Illinois;

- USP Leavenworth, Leavenworth, Kansas;

- USP Lompoc, Lompoc, California;

- USP Marion, Marion, Illinois;

- FCI Milan, Milan, Michigan;

- FCI Morgantown, Morgantown, West Virginia;

- FPC Pensacola, Pensacola, Florida;

- FCI Safford, Safford, Arizona;

- FCI Sandstone, Sandstone, Minnesota;

- FPC Seymour Johnson, Goldsboro, North Carolina;

- USP Terre Haute, Terre Haute, Indiana; and

- FPC Yankton, Yankton, South Dakota.

We also examined reported data for the 82 institutions listed in the following table.

Institution	Security Level	Institution	Security Level
ADX Florence	Maximum	FCI Petersburg	Low
FCI Allenwood	Low	FCI Petersburg	Medium
FCI Allenwood	Medium	FCI Phoenix	Medium
FCI Ashland	Low	FCI Ray Brook	Medium
FCI Bastrop	Low	FCI Safford	Low
FCI Beaumont	Low	FCI Sandstone	Low
FCI Beaumont	Medium	FCI Schuylkill	Medium
FCI Beckley	Medium	FCI Seagoville	Low
FCI Big Spring	Low	FCI Sheridan	Medium
FCI Butner	Low	FCI Talladega	Medium
FCI Butner	Medium	FCI Tallahassee	Low
FCI Coleman	Low	FCI Terminal Island	Medium
FCI Coleman	Medium	FCI Texarkana	Low
FCI Cumberland	Medium	FCI Three Rivers	Medium
FCI Danbury	Low	FCI Tucson	Medium
FCI Dublin	Low	FCI Victorville	Medium
FCI Edgefield	Medium	FCI Waseca	Low
FCI El Reno	Medium	FCI Yazoo City	Low
FCI Elkton	Low	FPC Alderson	Minimum
FCI Englewood	Medium	FPC Allenwood	Minimum
FCI Estill	Medium	FPC Bryan	Minimum
FCI Fairton	Medium	FPC Duluth	Minimum
FCI Florence	Medium	FPC Eglin	Minimum
FCI Forrest City	Low	FPC Montgomery	Minimum
FCI Fort Dix	Low	FPC Nellis	Minimum
FCI Greenville	Medium	FPC Pensacola	Minimum
FCI Jesup	Medium	FPC Seymour Johnson	Minimum
FCI La Tuna	Low	FPC Yankton	Minimum
FCI Lompoc	Low	USP Allenwood	High
FCI Loretto	Low	USP Atlanta	High
FCI Manchester	Medium	USP Atwater	High
FCI Marianna	Medium	USP Beaumont	High
FCI McKean	Medium	USP Coleman	High
FCI Memphis	Medium	USP Florence	High
FCI Miami	Medium	USP Leavenworth	High
FCI Milan	Low	USP Lee	High
FCI Morgantown	Minimum	USP Lewisburg	High
FCI Oakdale	Medium	USP Lompoc	High
FCI Otisville	Medium	USP Marion	High
FCI Oxford	Medium	USP Pollock	High
FCI Pekin	Medium	USP Terre Haute	High

The 82 institutions include the ADX and all FCIs, FPCs, and USPs. We excluded the FDCs, FMCs, FTCs, MCCs, MCFPs, and MDCs because of the unique missions of these institutions.

To determine the percentage of the educational and occupational goals achieved, we obtained the Annual Program Report for Education and Recreation Services for FY 1999 through FY 2002 for each institution included in our audit. We compared the completion goals and outcomes reported for each institution's GED, ESL, ACE, parenting, and occupational programs and determined the percentage of goal achieved, which equates to the outcome divided by goal. Additionally, for FY 2002 we compared the National Strategic Plan performance indicator goal and outcome for the percent of inmates enrolled in one or more education programs for each institution and determined the percentage of goal obtained.

To determine the percentage of the CCC utilization targets achieved for each institution during FY 2000 through 2002, we obtained the total number of inmates transferred to a CCC and total number of inmates released directly to the community as reported in the BOP's Key Indicators system.[48] To calculate the CCC utilization rate for each institution, which equates to the number of inmates transferred to a CCC divided by the number of inmates transferred to a CCC plus the number of inmates released directly into the community. We then compared the CCC utilization rate for each institution to the BOP's goal for that security level and determined the percentage of the goal achieved which equates to the outcome divided by goal.

To determine the GED performance factor for each institution during FY 1999 through FY 2002, we obtained the total number of completions and withdrawals from the BOP's Key Indicators system. We then calculated the GED performance factor, which equates to completions divided by completions plus withdrawals. Additionally, to determine the GED performance factor based on voluntary withdrawals for each institution, we obtained the total number of completions and voluntary withdrawals from the BOP's Key Indicators system. We then calculated the GED performance factor, which equates to completions divided by completions plus voluntary withdrawals.

To determine the percentage of citizen inmates required to participate in the literacy program that have dropped out and are therefore not promotable above the maintenance pay grade for work programs, we obtained the percentage of GED Dropped Non-promotable (GED DN) from the BOP's Key Indicators system for FY 1999 through FY 2002. Additionally,

---

[48] The BOP, *Key Indicators, A Strategic Support System of the Federal Bureau of Prisons*, Volume 14, Number 1, January 2003.

to determine the percentage of noncitizen inmates required participate in the literacy program that have dropped out and are therefore not promotable above the maintenance pay grade for work programs, we obtained the percentage of Exempt GED Non-promotable (GED XN) from the BOP's Key Indicators system.

Finally, to determine the occupational technical and vocational performance factors for each institution during FY 1999 through FY 2002, we obtained the total number of completions and withdrawals from the BOP's Key Indicators system. We then calculated the occupational technical performance factor, which equates to completions divided by completions plus withdrawals.

ANALYSIS OF THE OCCUPATIONAL EDUCATION
GOALS AND OUTCOMES FY 2001 THROUGH FY 2002

For the institutions included in our audit, we reviewed the occupational goals and outcomes for FY 1999 through FY 2002 reported in each institution's Annual Program Report for Education and Recreation Services. (The BOP did not require its institutions to establish occupational goals for FY 2002 because of a change in the format of the Annual Program Report for Education and Recreation Services; however, we used the FY 2002 occupational projected outcomes reported in the FY 2001 Annual Program Report for Education and Recreation Services as the FY 2002 occupational goals for our analysis.)

The following schedules provide the details of our analysis of the occupational goals and outcomes reported by each institution in its Annual Program Report for Education and Recreation Services for FY 2001 through FY 2002. Those institutions for which the occupational goal and/or outcome is shown as "---" in the following schedules did not include a goal and/or outcome in their Annual Program Report for Education and Recreation Services. Further, unless noted otherwise, those institutions for which the occupational goal and/or outcome is shown as "N/A" did not submit an Program Report for Education and Recreation Services because the institution was not open and/or fully operational during the fiscal year.

Occupational Education Completion Goals and Outcomes FY 2001

Institution	Security Level	Goal[49]	Outcome	Percent of Occupational Goal Achieved[50]
FPC Yankton	Minimum	35	103	294.29%
FPC Montgomery	Minimum	100	282	282.00%
FPC Nellis	Minimum	7	10	142.86%
FPC Seymour Johnson	Minimum	10	11	110.00%
FCI Morgantown	Minimum	200	201	100.50%
FPC Duluth	Minimum	31	30	96.77%
FPC Allenwood	Minimum	50	45	90.00%
FPC Bryan	Minimum	214	181	84.58%
FPC Pensacola	Minimum	100	75	75.00%
FPC Alderson	Minimum	262	109	41.60%
FPC Eglin	Minimum	160	39	24.38%
FCI Fort Dix	Low	755	1,969	260.79%
FCI Lompoc	Low	245	444	181.22%
FCI Milan	Low	133	205	154.14%
FCI Loretto	Low	200	296	148.00%
FCI Sandstone	Low	40	52	130.00%
FCI Texarkana	Low	150	187	124.67%
FCI Yazoo City	Low	225	263	116.89%
FCI Bastrop	Low	250	289	115.60%
FCI Beaumont	Low	270	301	111.48%
FCI Dublin	Low	56	62	110.71%
FCI Forrest City	Low	50	55	110.00%
FCI Safford	Low	100	108	108.00%
FCI La Tuna	Low	225	235	104.44%
FCI Tallahassee	Low	183	183	100.00%
FCI Petersburg	Low	130	129	99.23%
FCI Ashland	Low	253	247	97.63%
FCI Big Spring	Low	628	593	94.43%
FCI Danbury	Low	217	185	85.25%
FCI Butner	Low	305	227	74.43%

---

[49] The BOP changed the format of its Annual Program Report for Education and Recreation Services in FY 2001. The current year goals are no longer included in the report. Therefore, for our analysis we used the FY 2001 goals reported in the FY 2000 Annual Program Report for Education and Recreation Services.

[50] The percentage of goal achieved is equal to the outcome divided by the goal.

Occupational Education Completion Goals and Outcomes FY 2001

Institution	Security Level	Goal[49]	Outcome	Percent of Occupational Goal Achieved[50]
FCI Allenwood	Low	90	59	65.56%
FCI Waseca	Low	69	24	34.78%
FCI Elkton	Low	260	82	31.54%
FCI Seagoville	Low	710	133	18.73%
FCI Schuylkill	Medium	125	271	216.80%
FCI Greenville	Medium	40	73	182.50%
FCI Fairton	Medium	200	330	165.00%
FCI Beckley	Medium	402	628	156.22%
FCI Talladega	Medium	100	154	154.00%
FCI Oxford	Medium	54	78	144.44%
FCI Cumberland	Medium	50	69	138.00%
FCI Marianna	Medium	125	172	137.60%
FCI Miami	Medium	143	189	132.17%
FCI Phoenix	Medium	160	194	121.25%
FCI Edgefield	Medium	180	214	118.89%
FCI Butner	Medium	140	160	114.29%
FCI El Reno	Medium	210	225	107.14%
FCI Memphis	Medium	158	152	96.20%
FCI Terminal Island	Medium	153	137	89.54%
FCI McKean	Medium	175	153	87.43%
FCI Jesup	Medium	170	147	86.47%
FCI Pekin	Medium	110	92	83.64%
FCI Tucson	Medium	30	24	80.00%
FCI Englewood	Medium	20	15	75.00%
FCI Three Rivers	Medium	151	112	74.17%
FCI Ray Brook	Medium	75	55	73.33%
FCI Florence	Medium	128	93	72.66%
FCI Beaumont	Medium	220	153	69.55%
FCI Estill	Medium	360	231	64.17%
FCI Otisville	Medium	200	108	54.00%
FCI Sheridan	Medium	475	256	53.89%
FCI Manchester	Medium	155	80	51.61%
FCI Allenwood	Medium	71	36	50.70%
FCI Oakdale	Medium	405	132	32.59%
FCI Petersburg	Medium	N/A	N/A	------
FCI Victorville	Medium	N/A	19	------
USP Lewisburg	High	160	258	161.25%
USP Terre Haute	High	40	64	160.00%
USP Atlanta	High	50	76	152.00%

Occupational Education Completion Goals and Outcomes FY 2001

Institution	Security Level	Goal[49]	Outcome	Percent of Occupational Goal Achieved[50]
USP Lompoc	High	245	336	137.14%
USP Leavenworth	High	32	28	87.50%
USP Allenwood	High	210	180	85.71%
USP Marion	High	150	126	84.00%
USP Beaumont	High	266	103	38.72%
USP Florence	High	245	51	20.82%
USP Atwater	High	N/A	N/A	------
USP Lee	High	N/A	N/A	------
USP Pollock	High	N/A	N/A	------
ADX Florence	Maximum	N/A[51]	N/A	------
FCC Coleman	N/A[52]	203	166	81.77%

---

[51] The ADX Florence is a maximum security institution. Because of the unique mission of the institution the ADX Florence does not offer occupational education programs.

[52] The FY 2001 occupational goals for FCI Coleman (Low Security), FCI Coleman (Medium Security), and USP Coleman were combined in a single FY 2000 Annual Program Report for Education and Recreation Services report for the Federal Correctional Complex, and the FY 2001 occupational outcomes were combined in a single FY 2001 report.

Occupational Education Completion Goals and Outcomes FY 2002

Institution	Security Level	Goal[53]	Outcome	Percent of Occupational Goal Achieved[54]
FPC Yankton	Minimum	20	111	555.00%
FPC Seymour Johnson	Minimum	25	34	136.00%
FPC Pensacola	Minimum	76	84	110.53%
FPC Duluth	Minimum	31	29	93.55%
FCI Morgantown	Minimum	260	222	85.38%
FPC Nellis	Minimum	10	8	80.00%
FPC Alderson	Minimum	137	105	76.64%
FPC Bryan	Minimum	232	161	69.40%
FPC Eglin	Minimum	44	26	59.09%
FPC Allenwood	Minimum	49	N/A[55]	------
FPC Montgomery	Minimum	---	153	------
FCI Waseca	Low	27	61	225.93%
FCI Texarkana	Low	142	190	133.80%
FCI Sandstone	Low	36	47	130.56%
FCI Danbury	Low	202	253	125.25%
FCI Safford	Low	125	134	107.20%
FCI Forrest City	Low	32	34	106.25%
FCI Fort Dix	Low	652	685	105.06%
FCI Petersburg	Low	146	153	104.79%
FCI Elkton	Low	41	41	100.00%
FCI Bastrop	Low	330	326	98.79%
FCI Beaumont	Low	321	316	98.44%
FCI Allenwood	Low	111	104	93.69%
FCI Big Spring	Low	538	494	91.82%
FCI Tallahassee	Low	207	185	89.37%
FCI Dublin	Low	118	103	87.29%
FCI Butner	Low	253	203	80.24%
FCI Lompoc	Low	575	454	78.96%
FCI Seagoville	Low	169	132	78.11%
FCI Milan	Low	227	175	77.09%

[53] The BOP changed the format of its Annual Program Report for Education and Recreation Services in FY 2001. The current year goals are no longer included in the report. Further, the BOP did not require its institutions to establish goals for FY 2002. Therefore, for our analysis we used the FY 2002 projected outcomes reported in the FY 2001 Annual Program Report for Education and Recreation Services.

[54] The percentage of goal achieved is equal to the outcome divided by the goal.

[55] The FPC Allenwood did not submit a FY 2002 Annual Program Report for Education and Recreation Services because the institution was merged with FCI Allenwood (Medium) in FY 2002.

Occupational Education Completion Goals and Outcomes FY 2002

Institution	Security Level	Goal[53]	Outcome	Percent of Occupational Goal Achieved[54]
FCI Loretto	Low	260	84	32.31%
FCI Ashland	Low	256	82	32.03%
FCI La Tuna	Low	296	71	23.99%
FCI Yazoo City	Low	242	55	22.73%
FCI Tucson	Medium	20	43	215.00%
FCI Miami	Medium	215	435	202.33%
FCI Oxford	Medium	82	163	198.78%
FCI Sheridan	Medium	304	429	141.12%
FCI McKean	Medium	132	166	125.76%
FCI Cumberland	Medium	82	96	117.07%
FCI Estill	Medium	222	250	112.61%
FCI Florence	Medium	97	107	110.31%
FCI Butner	Medium	150	161	107.33%
FCI Talladega	Medium	125	132	105.60%
FCI Phoenix	Medium	196	191	97.45%
FCI Beaumont	Medium	191	180	94.24%
FCI Victorville	Medium	80	73	91.25%
FCI Pekin	Medium	72	64	88.89%
FCI El Reno	Medium	235	205	87.23%
FCI Allenwood	Medium	97	84	86.60%
FCI Three Rivers	Medium	136	111	81.62%
FCI Terminal Island	Medium	212	170	80.19%
FCI Fairton	Medium	371	294	79.25%
FCI Oakdale	Medium	152	115	75.66%
FCI Englewood	Medium	64	48	75.00%
FCI Ray Brook	Medium	54	39	72.22%
FCI Marianna	Medium	235	160	68.09%
FCI Beckley	Medium	392	256	65.31%
FCI Otisville	Medium	196	121	61.73%
FCI Greenville	Medium	227	116	51.10%
FCI Jesup	Medium	163	81	49.69%
FCI Manchester	Medium	135	64	47.41%
FCI Schuylkill	Medium	310	98	31.61%
FCI Edgefield	Medium	249	54	21.69%
FCI Memphis	Medium	---	220	------
FCI Petersburg	Medium	N/A	N/A	------
USP Beaumont	High	110	236	214.55%
USP Terre Haute	High	60	127	211.67%
USP Leavenworth	High	52	68	130.77%
USP Atlanta	High	99	77	77.78%
USP Pollock	High	120	81	67.50%
USP Allenwood	High	202	126	62.38%
USP Lompoc	High	414	207	50.00%

Occupational Education Completion Goals and Outcomes FY 2002

Institution	Security Level	Goal[53]	Outcome	Percent of Occupational Goal Achieved[54]
USP Lewisburg	High	351	174	49.57%
USP Florence	High	56	7	12.50%
USP Marion	High	125	14	11.20%
USP Atwater	High	N/A	N/A	------
USP Lee	High	N/A	0	------
ADX Florence	Maximum	N/A[56]	N/A	------
FCC Coleman	N/A[57]	178	239	134.27%

---

[56] The ADX Florence is a maximum security institution. Because of the unique mission of the institution the ADX Florence does not offer occupational education programs.

[57] The FY 2002 occupational projected outcomes for FCI Coleman (Low Security), FCI Coleman (Medium Security), and USP Coleman were combined in a single FY 2001 Annual Program Report for Education and Recreation Services report for the Federal Correctional Complex and the FY 2002 occupational outcomes were combined in a single FY 2002 report.

ANALYSIS OF THE GED GOALS AND OUTCOMES
FY 2001

For the institutions included in our audit, we reviewed the GED goals and outcomes for FY 1999 through FY 2001 reported in each institution's Annual Program Report for Education and Recreation Services. (The BOP did not require its institutions to establish GED goals for FY 2002 because of a change in the GED testing format that was implemented at the beginning of calendar year 2002.)

The following schedule provides the details of our analysis of the GED goals and outcomes reported by each institution in its Annual Program Report for Education and Recreation Services for FY 2001. Those institutions for which the GED goal and/or outcome is shown as "---" in the following schedules did not include a goal and/or outcome in their Annual Program Report for Education and Recreation Services. Further, unless noted otherwise, those institutions for which the GED goal and/or outcome is shown as "N/A" did not submit an Program Report for Education and Recreation Services because the institution was not open and/or fully operational during the fiscal year.

GED Completion Goals and Outcomes FY 2001

Institution	Security Level	Goal[58]	Outcome	Percent of GED Goal Achieved[59]
FPC Nellis	Minimum	35	63	180.00%
FPC Eglin	Minimum	30	46	153.33%
FPC Alderson	Minimum	50	71	142.00%
FPC Montgomery	Minimum	56	59	105.36%
FPC Bryan	Minimum	120	121	100.83%
FPC Seymour Johnson	Minimum	35	34	97.14%
FCI Morgantown	Minimum	70	64	91.43%
FPC Pensacola	Minimum	40	35	87.50%
FPC Duluth	Minimum	60	51	85.00%
FPC Yankton	Minimum	60	45	75.00%
FPC Allenwood	Minimum	125	48	38.40%
FCI Loretto	Low	55	89	161.82%
FCI Texarkana	Low	50	80	160.00%
FCI Butner	Low	50	66	132.00%
FCI Elkton	Low	77	97	125.97%
FCI Bastrop	Low	45	54	120.00%
FCI Sandstone	Low	40	46	115.00%
FCI Petersburg	Low	40	45	112.50%
FCI Safford	Low	70	78	111.43%
FCI Tallahassee	Low	80	89	111.25%
FCI Lompoc	Low	120	133	110.83%
FCI Seagoville	Low	45	47	104.44%
FCI Dublin	Low	75	77	102.67%
FCI Forrest City	Low	150	147	98.00%
FCI Waseca	Low	90	88	97.78%
FCI Allenwood	Low	70	66	94.29%
FCI Yazoo City	Low	85	75	88.24%
FCI Fort Dix	Low	240	200	83.33%
FCI Beaumont	Low	75	60	80.00%
FCI La Tuna	Low	110	86	78.18%
FCI Milan	Low	100	78	78.00%
FCI Big Spring	Low	50	37	74.00%
FCI Ashland	Low	100	70	70.00%
FCI Danbury	Low	100	29	29.00%

---

[58] The BOP changed the format of its Annual Program Report for Education and Recreation Services in FY 2001. The current year goals are no longer included in the report. Therefore, for our analysis we used the FY 2001 goals reported in the FY 2000 Annual Program Report for Education and Recreation Services.

[59] The percentage of goal achieved is equal to the outcome divided by the goal.

GED Completion Goals and Outcomes FY 2001

Institution	Security Level	Goal[58]	Outcome	Percent of GED Goal Achieved[59]
FCI Tucson	Medium	5	53	1,060.00%
FCI Miami	Medium	40	92	230.00%
FCI Talladega	Medium	65	97	149.23%
FCI El Reno	Medium	75	111	148.00%
FCI Cumberland	Medium	60	82	136.67%
FCI Florence	Medium	110	149	135.45%
FCI Marianna	Medium	50	66	132.00%
FCI Sheridan	Medium	80	104	130.00%
FCI Oakdale	Medium	35	45	128.57%
FCI Greenville	Medium	80	99	123.75%
FCI Three Rivers	Medium	70	85	121.43%
FCI Estill	Medium	50	59	118.00%
FCI Fairton	Medium	50	58	116.00%
FCI Beckley	Medium	110	122	110.91%
FCI McKean	Medium	75	83	110.67%
FCI Allenwood	Medium	60	64	106.67%
FCI Ray Brook	Medium	65	69	106.15%
FCI Pekin	Medium	70	74	105.71%
FCI Manchester	Medium	120	125	104.17%
FCI Oxford	Medium	65	65	100.00%
FCI Schuylkill	Medium	75	75	100.00%
FCI Victorville	Medium	65	65	100.00%
FCI Phoenix	Medium	75	73	97.33%
FCI Jesup	Medium	85	81	95.29%
FCI Memphis	Medium	146	134	91.78%
FCI Edgefield	Medium	70	63	90.00%
FCI Butner	Medium	60	51	85.00%
FCI Englewood	Medium	50	39	78.00%
FCI Otisville	Medium	100	74	74.00%
FCI Terminal Island	Medium	100	62	62.00%
FCI Beaumont	Medium	90	53	58.89%
FCI Petersburg	Medium	N/A	N/A	-------
USP Terre Haute	High	30	90	300.00%
USP Allenwood	High	25	29	116.00%
USP Beaumont	High	20	21	105.00%
USP Leavenworth	High	80	84	105.00%
USP Atlanta	High	100	100	100.00%
USP Marion	High	33	31	93.94%
USP Florence	High	32	27	84.38%
USP Lewisburg	High	90	67	74.44%
USP Lompoc	High	80	49	61.25%
USP Atwater	High	N/A	N/A	-------
USP Lee	High	N/A	N/A	-------
USP Pollock	High	N/A	16	-------

GED Completion Goals and Outcomes FY 2001

Institution	Security Level	Goal[58]	Outcome	Percent of GED Goal Achieved[59]
ADX Florence	Maximum	4	7	175.00%
FCC Coleman	N/A[60]	200	237	118.50%

---

[60] The FY 2001 GED goals for FCI Coleman (Low Security), FCI Coleman (Medium Security), and USP Coleman were combined in a single FY 2000 Annual Program Report for Education and Recreation Services report for the Federal Correctional Complex and the FY 2001 GED outcomes were combined in a single FY 2001 report.

ANALYSIS OF THE ESL GOALS AND OUTCOMES
FY 2001 THROUGH FY 2002

For the institutions included in our audit, we reviewed the ESL goals and outcomes for FY 1999 through FY 2002 reported in each institution's Annual Program Report for Education and Recreation Services. (The BOP did not require its institutions to establish ESL goals for FY 2002 because of a change in the format of the Annual Program Report for Education and Recreation Services; however, we used the FY 2002 ESL projected outcomes reported in the FY 2001 Annual Program Report for Education and Recreation Services as the FY 2002 ESL goals for our analysis.)

The following schedules provide the details of our analysis of the ESL goals and outcomes reported by each institution in its Annual Program Report for Education and Recreation Services for FY 2001 through FY 2002. Those institutions for which the ESL goal and/or outcome is shown as "---" in the following schedules did not include a goal and/or outcome in their Annual Program Report for Education and Recreation Services. Further, unless noted otherwise, those institutions for which the ESL goal and/or outcome is shown as "N/A" did not submit an Program Report for Education and Recreation Services because the institution was not open and/or fully operational during the fiscal year.

ESL Completion Goals and Outcomes FY 2001

Institution	Security Level	Goal[61]	Outcome	Percent of ESL Goal Achieved[62]
FPC Bryan	Minimum	7	22	314.29%
FPC Allenwood	Minimum	5	9	180.00%
FPC Montgomery	Minimum	10	17	170.00%
FPC Pensacola	Minimum	10	17	170.00%
FPC Yankton	Minimum	3	4	133.33%
FPC Eglin	Minimum	11	12	109.09%
FPC Alderson	Minimum	1	1	100.00%
FPC Duluth	Minimum	1	0	0.00%
FCI Morgantown	Minimum	1	0	0.00%
FPC Nellis	Minimum	4	0	0.00%
FPC Seymour Johnson	Minimum	1	0	0.00%
FCI Tallahassee	Low	35	52	148.57%
FCI Seagoville	Low	15	22	146.67%
FCI Elkton	Low	40	50	125.00%
FCI Loretto	Low	20	25	125.00%
FCI Safford	Low	20	25	125.00%
FCI Texarkana	Low	60	74	123.33%
FCI La Tuna	Low	40	44	110.00%
FCI Fort Dix	Low	80	87	108.75%
FCI Waseca	Low	30	29	96.67%
FCI Allenwood	Low	45	36	80.00%
FCI Sandstone	Low	10	7	70.00%
FCI Petersburg	Low	15	10	66.67%
FCI Yazoo City	Low	40	26	65.00%
FCI Forrest City	Low	45	26	57.78%
FCI Big Spring	Low	50	28	56.00%
FCI Butner	Low	10	5	50.00%
FCI Lompoc	Low	70	33	47.14%
FCI Bastrop	Low	20	9	45.00%
FCI Beaumont	Low	30	13	43.33%
FCI Dublin	Low	20	8	40.00%
FCI Danbury	Low	30	9	30.00%
FCI Ashland	Low	20	4	20.00%
FCI Milan	Low	5	0	0.00%

---

[61] The BOP changed the format of its Annual Program Report for Education and Recreation Services in FY 2001. The current year goals are no longer included in the report. Therefore, for our analysis we used the FY 2001 goals reported in the FY 2000 Annual Program Report for Education and Recreation Services.

[62] The percentage of goal achieved is equal to the outcome divided by the goal.

ESL Completion Goals and Outcomes FY 2001

Institution	Security Level	Goal[61]	Outcome	Percent of ESL Goal Achieved[62]
FCI Talladega	Medium	5	11	220.00%
FCI Sheridan	Medium	10	19	190.00%
FCI Oakdale	Medium	30	48	160.00%
FCI El Reno	Medium	10	13	130.00%
FCI Pekin	Medium	10	12	120.00%
FCI McKean	Medium	5	6	120.00%
FCI Florence	Medium	25	29	116.00%
FCI Manchester	Medium	12	13	108.33%
FCI Phoenix	Medium	20	20	100.00%
FCI Jesup	Medium	15	14	93.33%
FCI Ray Brook	Medium	15	14	93.33%
FCI Otisville	Medium	25	22	88.00%
FCI Terminal Island	Medium	20	16	80.00%
FCI Allenwood	Medium	15	12	80.00%
FCI Butner	Medium	5	4	80.00%
FCI Memphis	Medium	35	27	77.14%
FCI Cumberland	Medium	15	11	73.33%
FCI Beckley	Medium	10	7	70.00%
FCI Greenville	Medium	10	6	60.00%
FCI Estill	Medium	5	3	60.00%
FCI Miami	Medium	15	8	53.33%
FCI Three Rivers	Medium	20	10	50.00%
FCI Oxford	Medium	6	3	50.00%
FCI Victorville	Medium	25	12	48.00%
FCI Marianna	Medium	15	7	46.67%
FCI Englewood	Medium	30	12	40.00%
FCI Beaumont	Medium	30	8	26.67%
FCI Edgefield	Medium	8	1	12.50%
FCI Fairton	Medium	10	1	10.00%
FCI Schuylkill	Medium	15	1	6.67%
FCI Tucson	Medium	1	0	0.00%
FCI Petersburg	Medium	N/A	N/A	------
USP Terre Haute	High	10	15	150.00%
USP Lompoc	High	15	9	60.00%
USP Lewisburg	High	10	6	60.00%
USP Allenwood	High	5	3	60.00%
USP Atlanta	High	10	4	40.00%
USP Leavenworth	High	10	4	40.00%
USP Florence	High	15	2	13.33%
USP Beaumont	High	3	0	0.00%
USP Marion	High	2	0	0.00%
USP Pollock	High	N/A	1	------
USP Atwater	High	N/A	N/A	------
USP Lee	High	N/A	N/A	------

ESL Completion Goals and Outcomes FY 2001

Institution	Security Level	Goal[61]	Outcome	Percent of ESL Goal Achieved[62]
ADX Florence	Maximum	1	0	0.00%
FCC Coleman	N/A[63]	45	107	237.78%

---

[63] The FY 2001 ESL goals for FCI Coleman (Low Security), FCI Coleman (Medium Security), and USP Coleman were combined in a single FY 2000 Annual Program Report for Education and Recreation Services report for the Federal Correctional Complex and the FY 2001 ESL outcomes were combined in a single FY 2001 report.

ESL Completion Goals and Outcomes FY 2002

Institution	Security Level	Goal[64]	Outcome	Percent of ESL Goal Achieved[65]
FPC Eglin	Minimum	12	17	141.67%
FPC Alderson	Minimum	3	3	100.00%
FPC Bryan	Minimum	25	6	24.00%
FPC Pensacola	Minimum	20	4	20.00%
FPC Duluth	Minimum	1	0	0.00%
FPC Montgomery	Minimum	---	18	------
FPC Yankton	Minimum	---	1	------
FCI Morgantown	Minimum	---	0	------
FPC Nellis	Minimum	---	0	------
FPC Seymour Johnson	Minimum	---	0	------
FPC Allenwood	Minimum	8	N/A[66]	------
FCI Safford	Low	25	41	164.00%
FCI Waseca	Low	30	42	140.00%
FCI Dublin	Low	10	14	140.00%
FCI Big Spring	Low	35	44	125.71%
FCI Texarkana	Low	60	72	120.00%
FCI Loretto	Low	20	24	120.00%
FCI Lompoc	Low	50	53	106.00%
FCI Petersburg	Low	10	9	90.00%
FCI Danbury	Low	15	13	86.67%
FCI La Tuna	Low	50	40	80.00%
FCI Yazoo City	Low	35	28	80.00%
FCI Fort Dix	Low	100	79	79.00%
FCI Forrest City	Low	25	19	76.00%
FCI Seagoville	Low	30	22	73.33%
FCI Butner	Low	15	11	73.33%
FCI Bastrop	Low	15	8	53.33%
FCI Tallahassee	Low	40	21	52.50%
FCI Elkton	Low	45	23	51.11%
FCI Allenwood	Low	40	15	37.50%
FCI Sandstone	Low	10	3	30.00%

[64] The BOP changed the format of its Annual Program Report for Education and Recreation Services in FY 2001. The current year goals are no longer included in the report. Further, the BOP did not require its institutions to establish goals for FY 2002. Therefore, for our analysis we used the FY 2002 projected outcomes reported in the FY 2001 Annual Program Report for Education and Recreation Services.

[65] The percentage of goal achieved is equal to the outcome divided by the goal.

[66] The FPC Allenwood did not submit a FY 2002 Annual Program Report for Education and Recreation Services because the institution was merged with FCI Allenwood (Medium) in FY 2002.

ESL Completion Goals and Outcomes FY 2002

Institution	Security Level	Goal[64]	Outcome	Percent of ESL Goal Achieved[65]
FCI Beaumont	Low	30	7	23.33%
FCI Ashland	Low	5	0	0.00%
FCI Milan	Low	---	0	------
FCI Three Rivers	Medium	12	23	191.67%
FCI Miami	Medium	30	55	183.33%
FCI Greenville	Medium	4	6	150.00%
FCI Allenwood	Medium	12	16	133.33%
FCI Phoenix	Medium	20	24	120.00%
FCI Beaumont	Medium	5	6	120.00%
FCI Ray Brook	Medium	4	4	100.00%
FCI Florence	Medium	28	27	96.43%
FCI Sheridan	Medium	40	36	90.00%
FCI El Reno	Medium	15	12	80.00%
FCI Englewood	Medium	10	7	70.00%
FCI Cumberland	Medium	15	10	66.67%
FCI Fairton	Medium	3	2	66.67%
FCI Marianna	Medium	8	5	62.50%
FCI Jesup	Medium	15	8	53.33%
FCI Talladega	Medium	10	5	50.00%
FCI Otisville	Medium	20	9	45.00%
FCI Terminal Island	Medium	20	8	40.00%
FCI Oakdale	Medium	25	8	32.00%
FCI Victorville	Medium	30	6	20.00%
FCI Schuylkill	Medium	10	2	20.00%
FCI Tucson	Medium	10	2	20.00%
FCI Beckley	Medium	28	5	17.86%
FCI Manchester	Medium	15	2	13.33%
FCI Pekin	Medium	15	1	6.67%
FCI Estill	Medium	5	0	0.00%
FCI Memphis	Medium	---	15	------
FCI McKean	Medium	---	5	------
FCI Oxford	Medium	---	1	------
FCI Butner	Medium	---	0	------
FCI Edgefield	Medium	---	0	------
FCI Petersburg	Medium	N/A	N/A	------
USP Lompoc	High	8	15	187.50%
USP Allenwood	High	5	7	140.00%
USP Terre Haute	High	20	25	125.00%
USP Pollock	High	4	3	75.00%
USP Florence	High	12	3	25.00%
USP Atlanta	High	4	0	0.00%
USP Atwater	High	1	0	0.00%
USP Beaumont	High	5	0	0.00%
USP Leavenworth	High	---	3	------

ESL Completion Goals and Outcomes FY 2002

Institution	Security Level	Goal[64]	Outcome	Percent of ESL Goal Achieved[65]
USP Lee	High	N/A	3	------
USP Marion	High	---	1	------
USP Lewisburg	High	10	---	------
ADX Florence	Maximum	---	0	------
FCC Coleman	N/A[67]	100	53	53.00%

[67] The FY 2002 ESL projected outcomes for FCI Coleman (Low Security), FCI Coleman (Medium Security), and USP Coleman were combined in a single FY 2001 Annual Program Report for Education and Recreation Services report for the Federal Correctional Complex and the FY 2002 ESL outcomes were combined in a single FY 2002 report.

ANALYSIS OF THE ACE GOALS AND OUTCOMES
FY 2001 THROUGH FY 2002

For the institutions included in our audit, we reviewed the ACE goals and outcomes for FY 1999 through FY 2002 reported in each institution's Annual Program Report for Education and Recreation Services. (The BOP did not require its institutions to establish ACE goals for FY 2002 because of a change in the format of the Annual Program Report for Education and Recreation Services; however, we used the FY 2002 ACE projected outcomes reported in the FY 2001 Annual Program Report for Education and Recreation Services as the FY 2002 ACE goals for our analysis.)

The following schedules provide the details of our analysis of the ACE goals and outcomes reported by each institution in its Annual Program Report for Education and Recreation Services for FY 2001 through FY 2002. Those institutions for which the ACE goal and/or outcome is shown as "---" in the following schedules did not include a goal and/or outcome in their Annual Program Report for Education and Recreation Services. Further, unless noted otherwise, those institutions for which the ACE goal and/or outcome is shown as "N/A" did not submit an Program Report for Education and Recreation Services because the institution was not open and/or fully operational during the fiscal year.

ACE Completion Goals and Outcomes FY 2001

Institution	Security Level	Goal[68]	Outcome	Percent of ACE Goal Achieved[69]
FPC Nellis	Minimum	160	454	283.75%
FPC Pensacola	Minimum	160	294	183.75%
FPC Bryan	Minimum	1,547	1,622	104.85%
FPC Yankton	Minimum	115	120	104.35%
FPC Allenwood	Minimum	800	808	101.00%
FPC Duluth	Minimum	650	591	90.92%
FPC Seymour Johnson	Minimum	150	113	75.33%
FPC Eglin	Minimum	260	188	72.31%
FCI Morgantown	Minimum	600	377	62.83%
FPC Alderson	Minimum	60	34	56.67%
FPC Montgomery	Minimum	1,275	152	11.92%
FCI Waseca	Low	120	1,004	836.67%
FCI Bastrop	Low	95	577	607.37%
FCI Allenwood	Low	1,100	1,894	172.18%
FCI La Tuna	Low	270	361	133.70%
FCI Butner	Low	170	225	132.35%
FCI Sandstone	Low	200	240	120.00%
FCI Safford	Low	600	674	112.33%
FCI Petersburg	Low	415	450	108.43%
FCI Milan	Low	500	528	105.60%
FCI Loretto	Low	350	362	103.43%
FCI Ashland	Low	400	397	99.25%
FCI Yazoo City	Low	700	694	99.14%
FCI Big Spring	Low	610	600	98.36%
FCI Danbury	Low	550	530	96.36%
FCI Beaumont	Low	1,400	1,323	94.50%
FCI Elkton	Low	850	788	92.71%
FCI Forrest City	Low	1,300	1,185	91.15%
FCI Texarkana	Low	211	190	90.05%
FCI Lompoc	Low	950	697	73.37%
FCI Seagoville	Low	1,120	716	63.93%

---

[68] The BOP changed the format of its Annual Program Report for Education and Recreation Services in FY 2001. The current year goals are no longer included in the report. Therefore, for our analysis we used the FY 2001 goals reported in the FY 2000 Annual Program Report for Education and Recreation Services.

[69] The percentage of goal achieved is equal to the outcome divided by the goal.

ACE Completion Goals and Outcomes FY 2001

Institution	Security Level	Goal[68]	Outcome	Percent of ACE Goal Achieved[69]
FCI Tallahassee	Low	250	154	61.60%
FCI Dublin	Low	150	84	56.00%
FCI Fort Dix	Low	500	215	43.00%
FCI Butner	Medium	95	398	418.95%
FCI Talladega	Medium	65	192	295.38%
FCI Schuylkill	Medium	570	1,116	195.79%
FCI Oakdale	Medium	1,000	1,907	190.70%
FCI Three Rivers	Medium	400	695	173.75%
FCI Sheridan	Medium	500	787	157.40%
FCI Estill	Medium	400	628	157.00%
FCI Victorville	Medium	400	620	155.00%
FCI Oxford	Medium	450	645	143.33%
FCI Ray Brook	Medium	360	445	123.61%
FCI Otisville	Medium	750	909	121.20%
FCI Memphis	Medium	925	1,105	119.46%
FCI Florence	Medium	458	532	116.16%
FCI Englewood	Medium	250	290	116.00%
FCI Greenville	Medium	650	749	115.23%
FCI Terminal Island	Medium	200	227	113.50%
FCI Edgefield	Medium	185	205	110.81%
FCI El Reno	Medium	1,000	1,067	106.70%
FCI Fairton	Medium	800	768	96.00%
FCI McKean	Medium	350	331	94.57%
FCI Pekin	Medium	500	470	94.00%
FCI Phoenix	Medium	300	279	93.00%
FCI Beaumont	Medium	600	544	90.67%
FCI Marianna	Medium	250	226	90.40%
FCI Allenwood	Medium	380	332	87.37%
FCI Beckley	Medium	2,200	1,912	86.91%
FCI Manchester	Medium	330	222	67.27%
FCI Tucson	Medium	30	16	53.33%
FCI Miami	Medium	400	211	52.75%
FCI Jesup	Medium	1,000	498	49.80%
FCI Cumberland	Medium	700	60	8.57%
FCI Petersburg	Medium	N/A	N/A	------
USP Terre Haute	High	141	424	300.71%
USP Leavenworth	High	340	576	169.41%
USP Allenwood	High	175	294	168.00%

ACE Completion Goals and Outcomes FY 2001

Institution	Security Level	Goal[68]	Outcome	Percent of ACE Goal Achieved[69]
USP Atlanta	High	50	69	138.00%
USP Marion	High	275	348	126.55%
USP Florence	High	132	121	91.67%
USP Lewisburg	High	500	456	91.20%
USP Beaumont	High	855	673	78.71%
USP Lompoc	High	125	68	54.40%
USP Pollock	High	N/A	87	------
USP Atwater	High	N/A	N/A	------
USP Lee	High	N/A	N/A	------
ADX Florence	Maximum	650	690	106.15%
FCC Coleman	N/A[70]	737	1,612	218.72%

---

[70] The FY 2001 ACE goals for FCI Coleman (Low Security), FCI Coleman (Medium Security), and USP Coleman were combined in a single FY 2000 Annual Program Report for Education and Recreation Services report for the Federal Correctional Complex and the FY 2001 ACE outcomes were combined in a single FY 2001 report.

ACE Completion Goals and Outcomes FY 2002

Institution	Security Level	Goal[71]	Outcome	Percent of ACE Goal Achieved[72]
FPC Pensacola	Minimum	80	196	245.00%
FPC Alderson	Minimum	68	151	222.06%
FPC Nellis	Minimum	454	813	179.07%
FPC Bryan	Minimum	1,700	1,608	94.59%
FPC Eglin	Minimum	195	164	84.10%
FCI Morgantown	Minimum	400	331	82.75%
FPC Duluth	Minimum	650	423	65.08%
FPC Seymour Johnson	Minimum	116	64	55.17%
FPC Yankton	Minimum	132	69	52.27%
FPC Montgomery	Minimum	---	150	------
FPC Allenwood	Minimum	1,024	N/A[73]	------
FCI Dublin	Low	75	234	312.00%
FCI Texarkana	Low	100	241	241.00%
FCI Loretto	Low	350	773	220.86%
FCI Butner	Low	250	453	181.20%
FCI Petersburg	Low	450	691	153.56%
FCI Yazoo City	Low	700	1,056	150.86%
FCI La Tuna	Low	430	563	130.93%
FCI Big Spring	Low	200	235	117.50%
FCI Lompoc	Low	700	822	117.43%
FCI Safford	Low	680	754	110.88%
FCI Beaumont	Low	1,360	1,471	108.16%
FCI Fort Dix	Low	232	238	102.59%
FCI Sandstone	Low	250	254	101.60%
FCI Allenwood	Low	1,900	1,891	99.53%
FCI Elkton	Low	800	794	99.25%
FCI Seagoville	Low	750	716	95.47%

---

[71] The BOP changed the format of its Annual Program Report for Education and Recreation Services in FY 2001. The current year goals are no longer included in the report. Further, the BOP did not require its institutions to establish goals for FY 2002. Therefore, for our analysis we used the FY 2002 projected outcomes reported in the FY 2001 Annual Program Report for Education and Recreation Services.

[72] The percentage of goal achieved is equal to the outcome divided by the goal.

[73] The FPC Allenwood did not submit a FY 2002 Annual Program Report for Education and Recreation Services because the institution was merged with FCI Allenwood (Medium) in FY 2002.

ACE Completion Goals and Outcomes FY 2002

Institution	Security Level	Goal[71]	Outcome	Percent of ACE Goal Achieved[72]
FCI Waseca	Low	700	519	74.14%
FCI Forrest City	Low	1,200	859	71.58%
FCI Tallahassee	Low	204	139	68.14%
FCI Bastrop	Low	600	407	67.83%
FCI Milan	Low	540	318	58.89%
FCI Danbury	Low	600	277	46.17%
FCI Ashland	Low	---	583	------
FCI Talladega	Medium	120	293	244.17%
FCI Oxford	Medium	248	568	229.03%
FCI Tucson	Medium	30	66	220.00%
FCI Butner	Medium	288	473	164.24%
FCI Jesup	Medium	475	769	161.89%
FCI Victorville	Medium	730	1,103	151.10%
FCI Pekin	Medium	500	753	150.60%
FCI Phoenix	Medium	300	449	149.67%
FCI Beaumont	Medium	600	894	149.00%
FCI Marianna	Medium	230	324	140.87%
FCI Oakdale	Medium	1,640	2,174	132.56%
FCI Schuylkill	Medium	1,200	1,527	127.25%
FCI Ray Brook	Medium	336	417	124.11%
FCI McKean	Medium	300	357	119.00%
FCI Terminal Island	Medium	230	272	118.26%
FCI Greenville	Medium	800	828	103.50%
FCI Englewood	Medium	290	292	100.69%
FCI Fairton	Medium	800	795	99.38%
FCI Florence	Medium	555	548	98.74%
FCI Otisville	Medium	876	852	97.26%
FCI Allenwood	Medium	400	387	96.75%
FCI El Reno	Medium	1,000	963	96.30%
FCI Three Rivers	Medium	710	663	93.38%
FCI Cumberland	Medium	70	60	85.71%
FCI Beckley	Medium	1,876	1,523	81.18%
FCI Sheridan	Medium	872	694	79.59%
FCI Estill	Medium	844	668	79.15%
FCI Edgefield	Medium	316	240	75.95%
FCI Miami	Medium	276	170	61.59%
FCI Memphis	Medium	---	1,007	------
FCI Manchester	Medium	---	153	------
FCI Petersburg	Medium	N/A	N/A	------

ACE Completion Goals and Outcomes FY 2002

Institution	Security Level	Goal[71]	Outcome	Percent of ACE Goal Achieved[72]
USP Leavenworth	High	300	442	147.33%
USP Terre Haute	High	430	620	144.19%
USP Florence	High	132	177	134.09%
USP Beaumont	High	600	759	126.50%
USP Lompoc	High	75	91	121.33%
USP Pollock	High	300	345	115.00%
USP Lewisburg	High	500	441	88.20%
USP Atlanta	High	100	57	57.00%
USP Marion	High	420	227	54.05%
USP Allenwood	High	275	100	36.36%
USP Atwater	High	200	29	14.50%
USP Lee	High	N/A	319	------
ADX Florence	Maximum	700	881	125.86%
FCC Coleman	N/A[74]	1,500	1,238	82.53%

[74] The FY 2002 ACE projected outcomes for FCI Coleman (Low Security), FCI Coleman (Medium Security), and USP Coleman were combined in a single FY 2001 Annual Program Report for Education and Recreation Services report for the Federal Correctional Complex and the FY 2002 ACE outcomes were combined in a single FY 2002 report.

ANALYSIS OF THE PARENTING GOALS AND OUTCOMES
FY 2001 THROUGH FY 2002

For the institutions included in our audit, we reviewed the parenting goals and outcomes for FY 1999 through FY 2002 reported in each institution's Annual Program Report for Education and Recreation Services. (The BOP did not require its institutions to establish parenting goals for FY 2002 because of a change in the format of the Annual Program Report for Education and Recreation Services; however, we used the FY 2002 parenting projected outcomes reported in the FY 2001 Annual Program Report for Education and Recreation Services as the FY 2002 parenting goals for our analysis.)

The following schedules provide the details of our analysis of the parenting goals and outcomes reported by each institution in its Annual Program Report for Education and Recreation Services for FY 2001 through FY 2002. Those institutions for which the parenting goal and/or outcome is shown as "---" in the following schedules did not include a goal and/or outcome in their Annual Program Report for Education and Recreation Services. Further, unless noted otherwise, those institutions for which the parenting goal and/or outcome is shown as "N/A" did not submit an Program Report for Education and Recreation Services because the institution was not open and/or fully operational during the fiscal year.

Parenting Completion Goals and Outcomes FY 2001

Institution	Security Level	Goal[75]	Outcome	Percent of Parenting Goal Achieved[76]
FPC Nellis	Minimum	20	167	835.00%
FPC Seymour Johnson	Minimum	25	61	244.00%
FPC Eglin	Minimum	25	44	176.00%
FPC Pensacola	Minimum	20	33	165.00%
FPC Montgomery	Minimum	30	37	123.33%
FCI Morgantown	Minimum	200	230	115.00%
FPC Bryan	Minimum	500	547	109.40%
FPC Alderson	Minimum	900	811	90.11%
FPC Duluth	Minimum	80	62	77.50%
FPC Yankton	Minimum	75	50	66.67%
FPC Allenwood	Minimum	200	102	51.00%
FCI Butner	Low	30	54	180.00%
FCI Safford	Low	50	88	176.00%
FCI Dublin	Low	500	797	159.40%
FCI Sandstone	Low	150	221	147.33%
FCI Bastrop	Low	220	318	144.55%
FCI Allenwood	Low	170	228	134.12%
FCI Waseca	Low	70	81	115.71%
FCI Texarkana	Low	70	74	105.71%
FCI Petersburg	Low	90	94	104.44%
FCI Milan	Low	95	96	101.05%
FCI Lompoc	Low	375	367	97.87%
FCI Beaumont	Low	195	189	96.92%
FCI Big Spring	Low	180	159	88.33%
FCI Loretto	Low	125	110	88.00%
FCI La Tuna	Low	220	183	83.18%
FCI Danbury	Low	100	78	78.00%
FCI Forrest City	Low	240	167	69.58%
FCI Yazoo City	Low	100	65	65.00%
FCI Tallahassee	Low	50	31	62.00%
FCI Elkton	Low	110	51	46.36%

[75] The BOP changed the format of its Annual Program Report for Education and Recreation Services in FY 2001. The current year goals are no longer included in the report. Therefore, for our analysis we used the FY 2001 goals reported in the FY 2000 Annual Program Report for Education and Recreation Services.

[76] The percentage of goal achieved is equal to the outcome divided by the goal.

Parenting Completion Goals and Outcomes FY 2001

Institution	Security Level	Goal[75]	Outcome	Percent of Parenting Goal Achieved[76]
FCI Seagoville	Low	55	21	38.18%
FCI Fort Dix	Low	120	45	37.50%
FCI Ashland	Low	600	180	30.00%
FCI Oakdale	Medium	50	219	438.00%
FCI Marianna	Medium	75	271	361.33%
FCI Florence	Medium	85	173	203.53%
FCI Miami	Medium	100	176	176.00%
FCI Cumberland	Medium	200	343	171.50%
FCI McKean	Medium	300	500	166.67%
FCI Allenwood	Medium	150	208	138.67%
FCI Victorville	Medium	150	208	138.67%
FCI Memphis	Medium	173	216	124.86%
FCI Butner	Medium	90	99	110.00%
FCI Manchester	Medium	100	108	108.00%
FCI Three Rivers	Medium	75	77	102.67%
FCI Schuylkill	Medium	250	253	101.20%
FCI Englewood	Medium	60	57	95.00%
FCI Oxford	Medium	65	61	93.85%
FCI Ray Brook	Medium	120	110	91.67%
FCI Phoenix	Medium	80	67	83.75%
FCI Otisville	Medium	300	243	81.00%
FCI Beckley	Medium	100	75	75.00%
FCI Tucson	Medium	60	45	75.00%
FCI Beaumont	Medium	150	107	71.33%
FCI Pekin	Medium	300	209	69.67%
FCI Jesup	Medium	120	83	69.17%
FCI Sheridan	Medium	120	83	69.17%
FCI Greenville	Medium	65	44	67.69%
FCI Edgefield	Medium	150	100	66.67%
FCI Fairton	Medium	250	139	55.60%
FCI Terminal Island	Medium	35	15	42.86%
FCI Talladega	Medium	70	29	41.43%
FCI Estill	Medium	125	19	15.20%
FCI El Reno	Medium	---	78	------
FCI Petersburg	Medium	N/A	N/A	------
USP Terre Haute	High	25	69	276.00%
USP Florence	High	30	45	150.00%
USP Marion	High	30	42	140.00%

Parenting Completion Goals and Outcomes FY 2001				
Institution	Security Level	Goal[75]	Outcome	Percent of Parenting Goal Achieved[76]
USP Lompoc	High	30	37	123.33%
USP Lewisburg	High	350	401	114.57%
USP Beaumont	High	60	65	108.33%
USP Allenwood	High	200	200	100.00%
USP Leavenworth	High	50	42	84.00%
USP Atlanta	High	100	67	67.00%
USP Pollock	High	N/A	20	------
USP Atwater	High	N/A	N/A	------
USP Lee	High	N/A	N/A	------
ADX Florence	Maximum	20	12	60.00%
FCC Coleman	N/A[77]	200	260	130.00%

---

[77] The FY 2001 parenting goals for FCI Coleman (Low Security), FCI Coleman (Medium Security), and USP Coleman were combined in a single FY 2000 Annual Program Report for Education and Recreation Services report for the Federal Correctional Complex and the FY 2001 parenting outcomes were combined in a single FY 2001 report.

Parenting Completion Goals and Outcomes FY 2002

Institution	Security Level	Goal[78]	Outcome	Percent of Parenting Goal Achieved[79]
FPC Alderson	Minimum	200	297	148.50%
FPC Yankton	Minimum	88	90	102.27%
FPC Duluth	Minimum	70	63	90.00%
FPC Seymour Johnson	Minimum	55	47	85.45%
FPC Eglin	Minimum	46	32	69.57%
FPC Bryan	Minimum	600	339	56.50%
FCI Morgantown	Minimum	200	83	41.50%
FPC Nellis	Minimum	167	55	32.93%
FPC Montgomery	Minimum	---	30	------
FPC Pensacola	Minimum	---	20	------
FPC Allenwood	Minimum	85	N/A[80]	------
FCI Fort Dix	Low	92	172	186.96%
FCI Petersburg	Low	94	152	161.70%
FCI Elkton	Low	75	116	154.67%
FCI Tallahassee	Low	40	61	152.50%
FCI Yazoo City	Low	70	103	147.14%
FCI Ashland	Low	447	641	143.40%
FCI Waseca	Low	81	113	139.51%
FCI Loretto	Low	60	83	138.33%
FCI Safford	Low	50	60	120.00%
FCI Sandstone	Low	200	235	117.50%
FCI Texarkana	Low	48	55	114.58%
FCI Big Spring	Low	160	161	100.63%
FCI Lompoc	Low	400	368	92.00%
FCI Allenwood	Low	230	205	89.13%
FCI Butner	Low	60	50	83.33%
FCI Dublin	Low	600	492	82.00%

[78] The BOP changed the format of its Annual Program Report for Education and Recreation Services in FY 2001. The current year goals are no longer included in the report. Further, the BOP did not require its institutions to establish goals for FY 2002. Therefore, for our analysis we used the FY 2002 projected outcomes reported in the FY 2001 Annual Program Report for Education and Recreation Services.

[79] The percentage of goal achieved is equal to the outcome divided by the goal.

[80] The FPC Allenwood did not submit a FY 2002 Annual Program Report for Education and Recreation Services because the institution was merged with FCI Allenwood (Medium) in FY 2002.

Parenting Completion Goals and Outcomes FY 2002

Institution	Security Level	Goal[78]	Outcome	Percent of Parenting Goal Achieved[79]
FCI Bastrop	Low	330	252	76.36%
FCI La Tuna	Low	225	153	68.00%
FCI Beaumont	Low	200	129	64.50%
FCI Danbury	Low	80	47	58.75%
FCI Milan	Low	105	61	58.10%
FCI Forrest City	Low	180	104	57.78%
FCI Seagoville	Low	40	21	52.50%
FCI Fairton	Medium	150	905	603.33%
FCI Otisville	Medium	100	350	350.00%
FCI Sheridan	Medium	25	75	300.00%
FCI El Reno	Medium	125	353	282.40%
FCI Jesup	Medium	97	213	219.59%
FCI Phoenix	Medium	50	101	202.00%
FCI Estill	Medium	40	78	195.00%
FCI Marianna	Medium	125	226	180.80%
FCI Ray Brook	Medium	64	112	175.00%
FCI Three Rivers	Medium	120	206	171.67%
FCI Greenville	Medium	72	102	141.67%
FCI Victorville	Medium	180	247	137.22%
FCI McKean	Medium	364	408	112.09%
FCI Allenwood	Medium	125	131	104.80%
FCI Florence	Medium	160	165	103.13%
FCI Oakdale	Medium	96	96	100.00%
FCI Beckley	Medium	144	129	89.58%
FCI Cumberland	Medium	400	343	85.75%
FCI Terminal Island	Medium	30	25	83.33%
FCI Schuylkill	Medium	275	228	82.91%
FCI Talladega	Medium	60	43	71.67%
FCI Butner	Medium	196	139	70.92%
FCI Beaumont	Medium	115	80	69.57%
FCI Englewood	Medium	60	40	66.67%
FCI Edgefield	Medium	172	113	65.70%
FCI Manchester	Medium	110	71	64.55%
FCI Miami	Medium	150	37	24.67%
FCI Tucson	Medium	30	7	23.33%
FCI Pekin	Medium	---	197	------
FCI Memphis	Medium	---	144	------
FCI Oxford	Medium	---	66	------

Parenting Completion Goals and Outcomes FY 2002

Institution	Security Level	Goal[78]	Outcome	Percent of Parenting Goal Achieved[79]
FCI Petersburg	Medium	N/A	N/A	------
USP Terre Haute	High	60	97	161.67%
USP Lewisburg	High	350	449	128.29%
USP Allenwood	High	200	243	121.50%
USP Atlanta	High	75	87	116.00%
USP Pollock	High	80	80	100.00%
USP Lompoc	High	45	39	86.67%
USP Marion	High	75	63	84.00%
USP Beaumont	High	72	59	81.94%
USP Florence	High	28	7	25.00%
USP Atwater	High	10	0	0.00%
USP Lee	High	N/A	56	------
USP Leavenworth	High	---	28	------
ADX Florence	Maximum	20	48	240.00%
FCC Coleman	N/A[81]	250	144	57.60%

---

[81] The FY 2002 parenting projected outcomes for FCI Coleman (Low Security), FCI Coleman (Medium Security), and USP Coleman were combined in a single FY 2001 Annual Program Report for Education and Recreation Services report for the Federal Correctional Complex and the FY 2002 parenting outcomes were combined in a single FY 2002 report.

ANALYSIS OF THE PERCENT PARTICIPATION
GOALS AND OUTCOMES
FY 2002

For the institutions included in our audit, we reviewed the percent of inmates enrolled in one or more education programs (percent participation) goals and outcomes for FY 2002, reported in each institution's Annual Program Report for Education and Recreation Services.[82] The institutions in conjunction with the regional offices establish their own percent participation goals.

The following schedule provides the details of our analysis of the percent participation goals and outcomes reported by each institution in its Annual Program Report for Education and Recreation Services for FY 2002. Those institutions for which the percent participation goal and/or outcome is shown as "---" in the following schedule did not include a goal and/or outcome in their Annual Program Report for Education and Recreation Services. Further, unless noted otherwise, those institutions for which the percent participation goal and/or outcome is shown as "N/A" did not submit an Annual Program Report for Education and Recreation Services because the institution was not open and/or fully operational during the fiscal year.

---

[82] FY 2002 was the first year that the BOP institutions were required to report the percent participation goals and outcomes in the Annual Program Report for Education and Recreation Services.

Percent Participation Goals and Outcomes FY 2002

Institution	Security Level	Goal	Outcome	Percentage of Goal Achieved[83]
FPC Eglin	Minimum	27.00%	27.00%	100.00%
FPC Pensacola	Minimum	50.00%	50.00%	100.00%
FPC Seymour Johnson	Minimum	38.00%	38.00%	100.00%
FPC Bryan	Minimum	60.00%	58.00%	96.67%
FCI Morgantown	Minimum	45.00%	43.00%	95.56%
FPC Yankton	Minimum	40.00%	38.00%	95.00%
FPC Duluth	Minimum	30.00%	28.00%	93.33%
FPC Nellis	Minimum	70.00%	16.00%	22.86%
FPC Alderson	Minimum	---	---	------
FPC Allenwood	Minimum	N/A[84]	N/A	------
FPC Montgomery	Minimum	---	---	------
FCI Big Spring	Low	42.00%	49.00%	116.67%
FCI Seagoville	Low	35.00%	39.00%	111.43%
FCI Ashland	Low	36.00%	40.00%	111.11%
FCI Lompoc	Low	47.00%	52.00%	110.64%
FCI Texarkana	Low	44.00%	47.00%	106.82%
FCI La Tuna	Low	38.00%	39.00%	102.63%
FCI Bastrop	Low	40.00%	41.00%	102.50%
FCI Danbury	Low	53.30%	54.00%	101.31%
FCI Beaumont	Low	43.00%	43.00%	100.00%
FCI Milan	Low	70.00%	70.00%	100.00%
FCI Petersburg	Low	51.00%	51.00%	100.00%
FCI Sandstone	Low	35.00%	35.00%	100.00%
FCI Elkton	Low	45.00%	43.00%	95.56%
FCI Tallahassee	Low	55.00%	52.00%	94.55%
FCI Loretto	Low	39.00%	35.00%	89.74%
FCI Butner	Low	38.00%	34.00%	89.47%
FCI Allenwood	Low	42.00%	37.00%	88.10%
FCI Forrest City	Low	47.00%	41.00%	87.23%
FCI Dublin	Low	60.00%	52.00%	86.67%
FCI Waseca	Low	35.00%	28.00%	80.00%
FCI Yazoo City	Low	40.00%	28.00%	70.00%

---

[83] The percentage of goal achieved is equal to the outcome divided by the goal.

[84] The FPC Allenwood did not submit a FY 2002 Annual Program Report for Education and Recreation Services because the institution was merged with FCI Allenwood (Medium) in FY 2002.

Percent Participation Goals and Outcomes FY 2002

Institution	Security Level	Goal	Outcome	Percentage of Goal Achieved[83]
FCI Fort Dix	Low	---	27.19%	------
FCI Safford	Low	---	42.00%	------
FCI Fairton	Medium	62.00%	82.00%	132.26%
FCI Beaumont	Medium	27.00%	33.00%	122.22%
FCI Jesup	Medium	35.00%	39.50%	112.86%
FCI Memphis	Medium	36.00%	40.00%	111.11%
FCI Miami	Medium	45.00%	49.00%	108.89%
FCI Oakdale	Medium	34.00%	36.70%	107.94%
FCI Greenville	Medium	33.00%	35.00%	106.06%
FCI Ray Brook	Medium	31.60%	33.40%	105.70%
FCI Englewood	Medium	36.00%	38.00%	105.56%
FCI Phoenix	Medium	40.00%	42.00%	105.00%
FCI Three Rivers	Medium	40.00%	42.00%	105.00%
FCI Oxford	Medium	40.00%	41.00%	102.50%
FCI Terminal Island	Medium	40.00%	41.00%	102.50%
FCI Edgefield	Medium	32.00%	32.00%	100.00%
FCI Manchester	Medium	42.00%	42.00%	100.00%
FCI McKean	Medium	35.00%	35.00%	100.00%
FCI Sheridan	Medium	35.00%	35.00%	100.00%
FCI Allenwood	Medium	41.70%	40.80%	97.84%
FCI Florence	Medium	34.00%	33.16%	97.53%
FCI El Reno	Medium	36.00%	35.00%	97.22%
FCI Pekin	Medium	35.00%	33.00%	94.29%
FCI Victorville	Medium	30.00%	28.25%	94.17%
FCI Marianna	Medium	35.00%	32.00%	91.43%
FCI Estill	Medium	46.00%	41.00%	89.13%
FCI Beckley	Medium	40.00%	35.00%	87.50%
FCI Schuylkill	Medium	40.00%	33.00%	82.50%
FCI Tucson	Medium	40.00%	31.00%	77.50%
FCI Talladega	Medium	35.00%	27.00%	77.14%
FCI Butner	Medium	46.00%	---	------
FCI Cumberland	Medium	---	2.90%	------
FCI Otisville	Medium	40.00%	---	------
FCI Petersburg	Medium	N/A	N/A	------
USP Marion	High	25.00%	30.00%	120.00%
USP Pollock	High	40.00%	40.70%	101.75%
USP Allenwood	High	32.00%	32.00%	100.00%
USP Atwater	High	23.00%	23.00%	100.00%
USP Terre Haute	High	35.00%	35.00%	100.00%

Percent Participation Goals and Outcomes FY 2002

Institution	Security Level	Goal	Outcome	Percentage of Goal Achieved[83]
USP Lewisburg	High	40.00%	37.00%	92.50%
USP Beaumont	High	34.00%	31.00%	91.18%
USP Lompoc	High	18.00%	16.00%	88.89%
USP Atlanta	High	30.00%	23.00%	76.67%
USP Leavenworth	High	27.00%	19.90%	73.70%
USP Florence	High	38.00%	28.00%	73.68%
USP Lee	High	---	36.00%	------
ADX Florence	Maximum	48.00%	47.00%	97.92%
FCC Coleman	N/A[85]	39.00%	39.00%	100.00%

---

[85] The percent participation goal and outcome for FCI Coleman (Low Security), FCI Coleman (Medium Security), and USP Coleman were combined in a single FY 2002 Annual Program Report for Education and Recreation Services report for the Federal Correctional Complex.

ANALYSIS OF THE OCCUPATIONAL TECHNICAL PERFORMANCE FACTORS FY 2001 THROUGH FY 2002

For the occupational technical programs at each institution, we calculated a program performance factor for FY 1999 through FY 2002, based on the number of completions divided by the number of completions plus total withdrawals for each fiscal year. (We used completion and withdrawal data that was reported in the BOP's Key Indicators system for occupational technical programs to calculate the performance factor.) The performance factor measures the percentage of inmates who complete the occupational technical programs as compared to the percentage of inmates who withdraw from the programs.[86]

The following schedules provide the details of our calculations and analysis of the occupational technical performance factor for FY 2001 through FY 2002. Unless noted otherwise, those institutions for which the completions and/or total withdrawals are shown as "N/A" were not open and/or fully operational during the fiscal year.

---

[86] The performance factors for the occupational technical programs included in the BOP's Key Indicators was calculated based on completions divided by completions plus total withdrawals for the fiscal year.

Occupational Technical Performance Factors FY 2001

Institution	Security Level	Completions	Total Withdrawals	Performance Factor[87]
FPC Duluth	Minimum	30	0	100.00%
FPC Alderson	Minimum	0	0	N/A
FPC Allenwood	Minimum	0	0	N/A
FPC Bryan	Minimum	0	0	N/A
FPC Eglin	Minimum	0	0	N/A
FPC Montgomery	Minimum	0	0	N/A
FCI Morgantown	Minimum	0	0	N/A
FPC Nellis	Minimum	0	0	N/A
FPC Pensacola	Minimum	0	0	N/A
FPC Seymour Johnson	Minimum	0	0	N/A
FPC Yankton	Minimum	0	0	N/A
FCI Beaumont	Low	301	0	100.00%
FCI Safford	Low	108	0	100.00%
FCI Butner	Low	59	2	96.72%
FCI Fort Dix	Low	1,392	62	95.74%
FCI Bastrop	Low	56	4	93.33%
FCI Seagoville	Low	228	31	88.03%
FCI La Tuna	Low	232	32	87.88%
FCI Lompoc	Low	252	42	85.71%
FCI Sandstone	Low	11	2	84.62%
FCI Waseca	Low	116	22	84.06%
FCI Big Spring	Low	593	130	82.02%
FCI Texarkana	Low	360	95	79.12%
FCI Milan	Low	17	5	77.27%
FCI Forrest City	Low	50	54	48.08%
FCI Allenwood	Low	0	7	0.00%
FCI Ashland	Low	0	0	N/A
FCI Coleman	Low	0	0	N/A
FCI Danbury	Low	0	0	N/A
FCI Dublin	Low	0	0	N/A
FCI Elkton	Low	0	0	N/A
FCI Loretto	Low	0	0	N/A
FCI Petersburg	Low	0	0	N/A
FCI Tallahassee	Low	0	0	N/A
FCI Yazoo City	Low	0	0	N/A

[87] Institutions that did not have an occupational technical program during the fiscal year are shown as N/A in the performance factor column.

Occupational Technical Performance Factors FY 2001

Institution	Security Level	Completions	Total Withdrawals	Performance Factor[87]
FCI Florence	Medium	20	0	100.00%
FCI Terminal Island	Medium	88	3	96.70%
FCI Otisville	Medium	130	7	94.89%
FCI Jesup	Medium	515	31	94.32%
FCI Butner	Medium	116	8	93.55%
FCI El Reno	Medium	171	23	88.14%
FCI Beaumont	Medium	153	27	85.00%
FCI Phoenix	Medium	101	31	76.52%
FCI Estill	Medium	49	16	75.38%
FCI Sheridan	Medium	261	120	68.50%
FCI Three Rivers	Medium	11	7	61.11%
FCI Pekin	Medium	53	43	55.21%
FCI Allenwood	Medium	0	0	N/A
FCI Beckley	Medium	0	0	N/A
FCI Coleman	Medium	0	0	N/A
FCI Cumberland	Medium	0	0	N/A
FCI Edgefield	Medium	0	0	N/A
FCI Englewood	Medium	0	0	N/A
FCI Fairton	Medium	0	0	N/A
FCI Greenville	Medium	0	0	N/A
FCI Manchester	Medium	0	0	N/A
FCI Marianna	Medium	0	0	N/A
FCI McKean	Medium	0	0	N/A
FCI Memphis	Medium	0	0	N/A
FCI Miami	Medium	0	0	N/A
FCI Oakdale	Medium	0	0	N/A
FCI Oxford	Medium	0	0	N/A
FCI Ray Brook	Medium	0	0	N/A
FCI Schuylkill	Medium	0	0	N/A
FCI Talladega	Medium	0	0	N/A
FCI Tucson	Medium	0	0	N/A
FCI Victorville	Medium	0	0	N/A
FCI Petersburg	Medium	N/A	N/A	------
USP Marion	High	123	0	100.00%
USP Florence	High	82	4	95.35%
USP Beaumont	High	263	75	77.81%
USP Pollock	High	0	4	0.00%
USP Terre Haute	High	0	1	0.00%
USP Allenwood	High	0	0	N/A

Occupational Technical Performance Factors FY 2001

Institution	Security Level	Completions	Total Withdrawals	Performance Factor[87]
USP Atlanta	High	0	0	N/A
USP Coleman	High	0	0	N/A
USP Leavenworth	High	0	0	N/A
USP Lewisburg	High	0	0	N/A
USP Lompoc	High	0	0	N/A
USP Atwater	High	N/A	N/A	------
USP Lee	High	N/A	N/A	------
ADX Florence	Maximum	0	0	N/A

Occupational Technical Performance Factors FY 2002

Institution	Security Level	Completions	Total Withdrawals	Performance Factor[88]
FPC Bryan	Minimum	14	0	100.00%
FPC Pensacola	Minimum	39	0	100.00%
FPC Duluth	Minimum	29	1	96.67%
FPC Seymour Johnson	Minimum	33	7	82.50%
FPC Yankton	Minimum	56	12	82.35%
FPC Alderson	Minimum	41	14	74.55%
FPC Allenwood	Minimum	0	0	N/A
FPC Eglin	Minimum	0	0	N/A
FPC Montgomery	Minimum	0	0	N/A
FCI Morgantown	Minimum	0	0	N/A
FPC Nellis	Minimum	0	0	N/A
FCI Ashland	Low	2	0	100.00%
FCI Beaumont	Low	314	0	100.00%
FCI Safford	Low	134	3	97.81%
FCI Butner	Low	242	22	91.67%
FCI Tallahassee	Low	75	11	87.21%
FCI Lompoc	Low	308	49	86.27%
FCI Loretto	Low	84	14	85.71%
FCI Big Spring	Low	495	95	83.90%
FCI Fort Dix	Low	192	39	83.12%
FCI Seagoville	Low	156	41	79.19%
FCI Milan	Low	26	7	78.79%
FCI Texarkana	Low	325	93	77.75%
FCI Sandstone	Low	13	4	76.47%
FCI La Tuna	Low	126	80	61.17%
FCI Waseca	Low	64	41	60.95%
FCI Forrest City	Low	32	27	54.24%
FCI Bastrop	Low	68	91	42.77%
FCI Allenwood	Low	1	16	5.88%
FCI Coleman	Low	0	0	N/A
FCI Danbury	Low	0	0	N/A
FCI Dublin	Low	0	0	N/A
FCI Elkton	Low	0	0	N/A
FCI Petersburg	Low	0	0	N/A
FCI Yazoo City	Low	0	0	N/A

[88] Institutions that did not have an occupational technical program during the fiscal year are shown as N/A in the performance factor column.

Occupational Technical Performance Factors FY 2002

Institution	Security Level	Completions	Total Withdrawals	Performance Factor[88]
FCI El Reno	Medium	157	0	100.00%
FCI Florence	Medium	22	0	100.00%
FCI Ray Brook	Medium	24	0	100.00%
FCI Beckley	Medium	296	2	99.33%
FCI Otisville	Medium	117	6	95.12%
FCI Jesup	Medium	490	32	93.87%
FCI Memphis	Medium	91	12	88.35%
FCI Oxford	Medium	106	15	87.60%
FCI Butner	Medium	144	23	86.23%
FCI Beaumont	Medium	179	30	85.65%
FCI Terminal Island	Medium	46	8	85.19%
FCI Phoenix	Medium	113	20	84.96%
FCI Victorville	Medium	12	3	80.00%
FCI Estill	Medium	161	41	79.70%
FCI Miami	Medium	44	12	78.57%
FCI Greenville	Medium	104	30	77.61%
FCI Sheridan	Medium	398	115	77.58%
FCI Marianna	Medium	90	36	71.43%
FCI Pekin	Medium	21	11	65.63%
FCI Edgefield	Medium	13	8	61.90%
FCI Three Rivers	Medium	2	2	50.00%
FCI Englewood	Medium	0	2	0.00%
FCI Schuylkill	Medium	0	4	0.00%
FCI Allenwood	Medium	0	0	N/A
FCI Coleman	Medium	0	0	N/A
FCI Cumberland	Medium	0	0	N/A
FCI Fairton	Medium	0	0	N/A
FCI Manchester	Medium	0	0	N/A
FCI McKean	Medium	0	0	N/A
FCI Oakdale	Medium	0	0	N/A
FCI Petersburg	Medium	0	0	N/A
FCI Talladega	Medium	0	0	N/A
FCI Tucson	Medium	0	0	N/A
USP Atlanta	High	26	0	100.00%
USP Lewisburg	High	119	0	100.00%
USP Allenwood	High	103	1	99.04%
USP Marion	High	69	7	90.79%
USP Pollock	High	125	32	79.62%
USP Beaumont	High	244	113	68.35%

Occupational Technical Performance Factors FY 2002

Institution	Security Level	Completions	Total Withdrawals	Performance Factor[88]
USP Leavenworth	High	27	25	51.92%
USP Florence	High	6	14	30.00%
USP Terre Haute	High	0	16	0.00%
USP Atwater	High	0	0	N/A
USP Coleman	High	0	0	N/A
USP Lee	High	0	0	N/A
USP Lompoc	High	0	0	N/A
ADX Florence	Maximum	0	0	N/A

ANALYSIS OF THE OCCUPATIONAL VOCATIONAL PERFORMANCE FACTORS FY 2001 THROUGH FY 2002

For the occupational vocational programs at each institution, we calculated a program performance factor for FY 1999 through FY 2002, based on the number of completions divided by the number of completions plus total withdrawals for each fiscal year. (We used completion and withdrawal data that was reported in the BOP's Key Indicators system for occupational vocational programs to calculate the performance factor.) The performance factor measures the percentage of inmates who complete the occupational vocational programs as compared to the percentage of inmates who withdraw from the programs.[89]

The following schedules provide the details of our analysis of the occupational vocational performance factor for FY 2001 through FY 2002. Unless noted otherwise, those institutions for which the completions and/or total withdrawals are shown as "N/A" were not open and/or fully operational during the fiscal year.

---

[89] The performance factors for the occupational technical programs included in the BOP's Key Indicators was calculated based on completions divided by completions plus total withdrawals for the fiscal year.

Occupational Vocational Performance Factors FY 2001

Institution	Security Level	Completions	Total Withdrawals	Performance Factor[90]
FPC Seymour Johnson	Minimum	11	0	100.00%
FPC Pensacola	Minimum	79	1	98.75%
FPC Yankton	Minimum	95	2	97.94%
FPC Bryan	Minimum	183	8	95.81%
FCI Morgantown	Minimum	201	9	95.71%
FPC Eglin	Minimum	196	12	94.23%
FPC Duluth	Minimum	12	1	92.31%
FPC Alderson	Minimum	229	31	88.08%
FPC Montgomery	Minimum	310	50	86.11%
FPC Allenwood	Minimum	45	9	83.33%
FPC Nellis	Minimum	2	2	50.00%
FCI Milan	Low	121	0	100.00%
FCI Safford	Low	65	0	100.00%
FCI Ashland	Low	238	3	98.76%
FCI Butner	Low	289	6	97.97%
FCI Loretto	Low	308	12	96.25%
FCI Bastrop	Low	238	12	95.20%
FCI Fort Dix	Low	560	41	93.18%
FCI Seagoville	Low	185	16	92.04%
FCI Lompoc	Low	192	18	91.43%
FCI Coleman	Low	93	11	89.42%
FCI Tallahassee	Low	208	28	88.14%
FCI Sandstone	Low	44	6	88.00%
FCI Texarkana	Low	36	6	85.71%
FCI Petersburg	Low	152	30	83.52%
FCI Yazoo City	Low	263	52	83.49%
FCI Forrest City	Low	5	1	83.33%
FCI Allenwood	Low	59	13	81.94%
FCI Danbury	Low	192	65	74.71%
FCI Elkton	Low	270	98	73.37%
FCI La Tuna	Low	2	1	66.67%
FCI Dublin	Low	288	146	66.36%
FCI Waseca	Low	31	23	57.41%
FCI Beaumont	Low	0	1	0.00%
FCI Big Spring	Low	0	2	0.00%

[90] Institutions that did not have an occupational vocational program during the fiscal year are shown as N/A in the performance factor column.

Occupational Vocational Performance Factors FY 2001

Institution	Security Level	Completions	Total Withdrawals	Performance Factor[90]
FCI Tucson	Medium	24	0	100.00%
FCI Beckley	Medium	414	5	98.81%
FCI Oakdale	Medium	289	6	97.97%
FCI El Reno	Medium	49	2	96.08%
FCI Coleman	Medium	116	8	93.55%
FCI Butner	Medium	26	2	92.86%
FCI Estill	Medium	182	18	91.00%
FCI Marianna	Medium	242	25	90.64%
FCI Edgefield	Medium	214	23	90.30%
FCI Talladega	Medium	149	16	90.30%
FCI Allenwood	Medium	61	7	89.71%
FCI Manchester	Medium	165	19	89.67%
FCI Schuylkill	Medium	102	13	88.70%
FCI Pekin	Medium	39	6	86.67%
FCI Fairton	Medium	309	48	86.55%
FCI Miami	Medium	302	48	86.29%
FCI Sheridan	Medium	81	13	86.17%
FCI Memphis	Medium	152	25	85.88%
FCI Cumberland	Medium	105	28	78.95%
FCI Ray Brook	Medium	55	16	77.46%
FCI McKean	Medium	306	108	73.91%
FCI Otisville	Medium	31	12	72.09%
FCI Victorville	Medium	43	20	68.25%
FCI Florence	Medium	73	34	68.22%
FCI Phoenix	Medium	93	44	67.88%
FCI Terminal Island	Medium	106	54	66.25%
FCI Greenville	Medium	73	38	65.77%
FCI Oxford	Medium	49	35	58.33%
FCI Jesup	Medium	2	2	50.00%
FCI Three Rivers	Medium	110	167	39.71%
FCI Englewood	Medium	16	99	13.91%
FCI Beaumont	Medium	0	6	0.00%
FCI Petersburg	Medium	N/A	N/A	------
USP Lompoc	High	333	12	96.52%
USP Lewisburg	High	260	11	95.94%
USP Terre Haute	High	70	10	87.50%
USP Allenwood	High	79	17	82.29%
USP Marion	High	3	1	75.00%
USP Atlanta	High	79	62	56.03%

Occupational Vocational Performance Factors FY 2001

Institution	Security Level	Completions	Total Withdrawals	Performance Factor[90]
USP Leavenworth	High	34	48	41.46%
USP Florence	High	36	55	39.56%
USP Beaumont	High	0	1	0.00%
USP Coleman	High	0	0	N/A
USP Pollock	High	0	0	N/A
USP Atwater	High	N/A	N/A	------
USP Lee	High	N/A	N/A	------
ADX Florence	Maximum	0	0	N/A

Occupational Vocational Performance Factors FY 2002

Institution	Security Level	Completions	Total Withdrawals	Performance Factor[91]
FPC Nellis	Minimum	8	0	100.00%
FPC Pensacola	Minimum	40	0	100.00%
FCI Morgantown	Minimum	250	8	96.90%
FPC Yankton	Minimum	47	2	95.92%
FPC Bryan	Minimum	133	6	95.68%
FPC Eglin	Minimum	140	7	95.24%
FPC Alderson	Minimum	188	23	89.10%
FPC Montgomery	Minimum	219	50	81.41%
FPC Allenwood	Minimum	42	27	60.87%
FPC Seymour Johnson	Minimum	1	1	50.00%
FPC Duluth	Minimum	0	3	0.00%
FCI Forrest City	Low	2	0	100.00%
FCI Safford	Low	81	1	98.78%
FCI Ashland	Low	157	2	98.74%
FCI Seagoville	Low	64	1	98.46%
FCI Butner	Low	190	3	98.45%
FCI Bastrop	Low	262	26	90.97%
FCI Sandstone	Low	37	4	90.24%
FCI Tallahassee	Low	129	14	90.21%
FCI Lompoc	Low	146	20	87.95%
FCI Milan	Low	147	22	86.98%
FCI Fort Dix	Low	620	102	85.87%
FCI Allenwood	Low	105	20	84.00%
FCI Yazoo City	Low	228	45	83.52%
FCI Coleman	Low	109	22	83.21%
FCI Elkton	Low	305	67	81.99%
FCI Loretto	Low	176	45	79.64%
FCI Petersburg	Low	142	45	75.94%
FCI Danbury	Low	195	85	69.64%
FCI Dublin	Low	303	165	64.74%
FCI Beaumont	Low	2	3	40.00%
FCI Texarkana	Low	14	23	37.84%
FCI Big Spring	Low	1	2	33.33%
FCI La Tuna	Low	0	1	0.00%

---

[91] Institutions that did not have an occupational vocational program during the fiscal year are shown as N/A in the performance factor column.

Occupational Vocational Performance Factors FY 2002

Institution	Security Level	Completions	Total Withdrawals	Performance Factor[91]
FCI Waseca	Low	0	7	0.00%
FCI Beckley	Medium	11	0	100.00%
FCI Butner	Medium	39	0	100.00%
FCI Tucson	Medium	43	0	100.00%
FCI Coleman	Medium	246	5	98.01%
FCI Memphis	Medium	123	4	96.85%
FCI Oakdale	Medium	428	26	94.27%
FCI Allenwood	Medium	102	8	92.73%
FCI Cumberland	Medium	151	13	92.07%
FCI Victorville	Medium	205	20	91.11%
FCI Pekin	Medium	46	5	90.20%
FCI Estill	Medium	119	16	88.15%
FCI Oxford	Medium	22	3	88.00%
FCI Fairton	Medium	270	41	86.82%
FCI Talladega	Medium	188	32	85.45%
FCI Miami	Medium	276	50	84.66%
FCI Terminal Island	Medium	122	23	84.14%
FCI Edgefield	Medium	139	27	83.73%
FCI Marianna	Medium	150	31	82.87%
FCI Manchester	Medium	117	25	82.39%
FCI Schuylkill	Medium	67	15	81.71%
FCI Florence	Medium	85	22	79.44%
FCI El Reno	Medium	46	12	79.31%
FCI Sheridan	Medium	34	9	79.07%
FCI McKean	Medium	247	75	76.71%
FCI Ray Brook	Medium	130	40	76.47%
FCI Otisville	Medium	73	32	69.52%
FCI Phoenix	Medium	58	58	50.00%
FCI Three Rivers	Medium	107	109	49.54%
FCI Englewood	Medium	49	85	36.57%
FCI Greenville	Medium	12	33	26.67%
FCI Beaumont	Medium	1	3	25.00%
FCI Jesup	Medium	0	0	N/A
FCI Petersburg	Medium	0	0	N/A
USP Lewisburg	High	176	4	97.78%
USP Lompoc	High	280	26	91.50%
USP Terre Haute	High	127	26	83.01%
USP Allenwood	High	23	6	79.31%

Occupational Vocational Performance Factors FY 2002

Institution	Security Level	Completions	Total Withdrawals	Performance Factor[91]
USP Pollock	High	23	8	74.19%
USP Atlanta	High	51	21	70.83%
USP Leavenworth	High	43	20	68.25%
USP Marion	High	6	8	42.86%
USP Beaumont	High	0	1	0.00%
USP Coleman	High	0	4	0.00%
USP Florence	High	0	66	0.00%
USP Atwater	High	0	0	N/A
USP Lee	High	0	0	N/A
ADX Florence	Maximum	0	0	N/A

ANALYSIS OF THE PERCENTAGE OF CITIZEN GED DROPPED NON-PROMOTABLE INMATES FY 2001 THROUGH FY 2002

For the institutions included in our audit, we reviewed the percentage of citizen inmates required to participate in the literacy program that have dropped out, and are therefore not promotable above the maintenance pay grade for work programs for FY 1999 through FY 2002. These inmates are designated as GED Dropped Non-promotable (GED DN) in the BOP's Key Indicators.

The following schedules provide the details of our analysis of the percentage of GED Dropped Non-promotable inmates as reported by the BOP in its Key Indicators for FY 2001 through FY 2002. Unless noted otherwise, those institutions for which the number of GED Dropped Non-promotable inmates is shown as "N/A" were not open and/or fully operational during the fiscal year.

GED Dropped Non-promotable FY 2001

Institution	Security Level	Number of Inmates GED Dropped Non-promotable	Percent of Inmates GED Dropped Non-promotable
FPC Duluth	Minimum	21	4.00%
FPC Seymour Johnson	Minimum	16	3.00%
FPC Eglin	Minimum	23	2.60%
FPC Allenwood	Minimum	18	2.40%
FPC Montgomery	Minimum	16	1.90%
FPC Pensacola	Minimum	10	1.90%
FPC Nellis	Minimum	9	1.60%
FPC Alderson	Minimum	10	1.20%
FCI Morgantown	Minimum	9	0.80%
FPC Bryan	Minimum	3	0.40%
FPC Yankton	Minimum	2	0.30%
FCI Petersburg	Low	65	4.10%
FCI Butner	Low	50	4.00%
FCI Yazoo City	Low	79	3.80%
FCI Sandstone	Low	29	3.60%
FCI Ashland	Low	42	3.00%
FCI Bastrop	Low	37	2.70%
FCI Beaumont	Low	50	2.60%
FCI Forrest City	Low	53	2.60%
FCI Allenwood	Low	33	2.50%
FCI Milan	Low	41	2.50%
FCI Danbury	Low	31	2.30%
FCI Coleman	Low	44	2.10%
FCI Fort Dix	Low	86	2.00%
FCI Elkton	Low	40	1.80%
FCI Loretto	Low	20	1.70%
FCI Texarkana	Low	25	1.60%
FCI Waseca	Low	16	1.50%
FCI Seagoville	Low	13	1.30%
FCI Tallahassee	Low	17	1.30%
FCI Dublin	Low	12	0.90%
FCI Big Spring	Low	7	0.80%
FCI La Tuna	Low	13	0.80%
FCI Safford	Low	6	0.70%
FCI Lompoc	Low	3	0.30%
FCI Edgefield	Medium	188	9.50%
FCI Memphis	Medium	126	8.60%
FCI Fairton	Medium	84	6.10%

GED Dropped Non-promotable FY 2001

Institution	Security Level	Number of Inmates GED Dropped Non-promotable	Percent of Inmates GED Dropped Non-promotable
FCI Miami	Medium	82	5.80%
FCI Estill	Medium	80	5.60%
FCI Schuylkill	Medium	83	5.60%
FCI Coleman	Medium	108	5.40%
FCI Oxford	Medium	60	5.30%
FCI Greenville	Medium	74	5.20%
FCI Marianna	Medium	75	5.20%
FCI Talladega	Medium	75	5.20%
FCI Butner	Medium	59	5.00%
FCI Otisville	Medium	51	4.80%
FCI Pekin	Medium	70	4.70%
FCI Cumberland	Medium	65	4.60%
FCI Manchester	Medium	78	4.60%
FCI Florence	Medium	72	4.40%
FCI McKean	Medium	60	4.20%
FCI Allenwood	Medium	49	3.80%
FCI Beaumont	Medium	60	3.80%
FCI Beckley	Medium	79	3.80%
FCI Englewood	Medium	37	3.50%
FCI Ray Brook	Medium	42	3.50%
FCI Jesup	Medium	61	3.40%
FCI Oakdale	Medium	38	3.10%
FCI Three Rivers	Medium	41	3.00%
FCI Sheridan	Medium	48	2.50%
FCI Victorville	Medium	46	2.40%
FCI El Reno	Medium	38	2.30%
FCI Phoenix	Medium	30	2.30%
FCI Tucson	Medium	14	1.60%
FCI Terminal Island	Medium	9	0.90%
FCI Petersburg	Medium	N/A	------
USP Beaumont	High	218	14.30%
USP Atlanta	High	281	12.30%
USP Leavenworth	High	241	11.00%
USP Florence	High	94	10.60%
USP Coleman	High	39	9.70%
USP Allenwood	High	110	9.60%
USP Terre Haute	High	120	7.00%
USP Marion	High	48	6.30%
USP Pollock	High	48	6.20%

GED Dropped Non-promotable FY 2001

Institution	Security Level	Number of Inmates GED Dropped Non-promotable	Percent of Inmates GED Dropped Non-promotable
USP Lewisburg	High	93	5.90%
USP Lompoc	High	99	5.80%
USP Atwater	High	N/A	------
USP Lee	High	N/A	------
ADX Florence	Maximum	60	15.70%

GED Dropped Non-promotable FY 2002

Institution	Security Level	Number of Inmates GED Dropped Non-promotable	Percent of Inmates GED Dropped Non-promotable
FPC Seymour Johnson	Minimum	25	4.50%
FPC Duluth	Minimum	17	2.90%
FPC Eglin	Minimum	21	2.70%
FPC Allenwood	Minimum	15	2.60%
FPC Pensacola	Minimum	11	2.30%
FPC Montgomery	Minimum	11	1.40%
FCI Morgantown	Minimum	12	1.10%
FPC Yankton	Minimum	5	0.80%
FPC Nellis	Minimum	4	0.70%
FPC Alderson	Minimum	6	0.60%
FPC Bryan	Minimum	2	0.20%
FCI Butner	Low	61	4.50%
FCI Petersburg	Low	60	4.10%
FCI Yazoo City	Low	68	3.30%
FCI Ashland	Low	45	3.10%
FCI Bastrop	Low	41	2.80%
FCI Forrest City	Low	57	2.80%
FCI Sandstone	Low	22	2.70%
FCI Fort Dix	Low	108	2.40%
FCI Allenwood	Low	32	2.30%
FCI Elkton	Low	55	2.30%
FCI Milan	Low	33	2.30%
FCI Beaumont	Low	39	1.90%
FCI Coleman	Low	39	1.90%
FCI Seagoville	Low	23	1.80%
FCI Texarkana	Low	29	1.80%
FCI Danbury	Low	22	1.70%
FCI Loretto	Low	18	1.50%
FCI Tallahassee	Low	20	1.50%
FCI Waseca	Low	10	1.00%
FCI Dublin	Low	12	0.80%
FCI La Tuna	Low	11	0.70%
FCI Big Spring	Low	6	0.60%
FCI Safford	Low	4	0.50%
FCI Lompoc	Low	4	0.30%
FCI Edgefield	Medium	118	8.30%
FCI Memphis	Medium	122	7.90%

GED Dropped Non-promotable FY 2002

Institution	Security Level	Number of Inmates GED Dropped Non-promotable	Percent of Inmates GED Dropped Non-promotable
FCI Schuylkill	Medium	113	7.50%
FCI Marianna	Medium	103	6.90%
FCI Estill	Medium	98	6.70%
FCI Cumberland	Medium	99	6.60%
FCI Miami	Medium	94	6.40%
FCI Talladega	Medium	90	6.30%
FCI Coleman	Medium	126	6.00%
FCI Otisville	Medium	66	6.00%
FCI Fairton	Medium	79	5.70%
FCI Manchester	Medium	93	5.60%
FCI Jesup	Medium	97	5.40%
FCI Oxford	Medium	62	5.40%
FCI Petersburg	Medium	65	5.40%
FCI Pekin	Medium	76	5.00%
FCI Greenville	Medium	66	4.50%
FCI Florence	Medium	75	4.40%
FCI Ray Brook	Medium	55	4.30%
FCI Butner	Medium	45	3.70%
FCI El Reno	Medium	49	3.60%
FCI Allenwood	Medium	46	3.40%
FCI Beaumont	Medium	57	3.40%
FCI Beckley	Medium	72	3.40%
FCI McKean	Medium	56	3.40%
FCI Three Rivers	Medium	43	3.20%
FCI Oakdale	Medium	35	2.70%
FCI Englewood	Medium	25	2.50%
FCI Victorville	Medium	41	2.20%
FCI Sheridan	Medium	35	1.90%
FCI Phoenix	Medium	24	1.70%
FCI Tucson	Medium	14	1.70%
FCI Terminal Island	Medium	6	0.60%
USP Beaumont	High	230	13.80%
USP Atlanta	High	324	12.40%
USP Florence	High	117	12.20%
USP Leavenworth	High	222	10.50%
USP Pollock	High	143	9.50%
USP Allenwood	High	98	9.40%
USP Coleman	High	150	9.20%

GED Dropped Non-promotable FY 2002

Institution	Security Level	Number of Inmates GED Dropped Non-promotable	Percent of Inmates GED Dropped Non-promotable
USP Lompoc	High	110	7.60%
USP Marion	High	58	7.40%
USP Lee	High	62	6.10%
USP Terre Haute	High	85	6.10%
USP Lewisburg	High	97	6.00%
USP Atwater	High	77	5.60%
ADX Florence	Maximum	53	13.00%

122

ANALYSIS OF THE CCC UTILIZATION
TARGETS AND OUTCOMES FY 2001 THROUGH 2002

For each institution included in our audit, we calculated the CCC utilization rate, for FY 2000 through FY 2002. To calculate the CCC utilization rate, we used the total number of inmates transferred to a CCC and total number of inmates released directly to the community as reported in the BOP's Key Indicators.[92] For the minimum, low and medium security institutions, we also compared the CCC utilization rate calculated for each institution to the CCC utilization target for the corresponding security level.

The following schedules provide the details of our calculations and analysis of the CCC utilization rates for FY 2001 through FY 2002. Unless noted otherwise, those institutions for which the CCC utilization outcome is shown as "N/A" did not submit an Program Report for Education and Recreation Services because the institution was not open and/or fully operational during the fiscal year.

---

[92] The CCC utilization rate is equal to the total number of inmates placed in a CCC prior to release divided by the total number of inmates released.

CCC Utilization Goals and Outcomes FY 2001

Institution	Security Level	Goal[93]	Outcome	Percent of CCC Utilization Goal Achieved[94]
FPC Yankton	Minimum	80.00%	94.41%	118.01%
FPC Nellis	Minimum	80.00%	93.90%	117.38%
FPC Montgomery	Minimum	80.00%	93.13%	116.41%
FCI Morgantown	Minimum	80.00%	91.93%	114.91%
FPC Bryan	Minimum	80.00%	89.89%	112.36%
FPC Pensacola	Minimum	80.00%	88.65%	110.81%
FPC Seymour Johnson	Minimum	80.00%	88.41%	110.51%
FPC Allenwood	Minimum	80.00%	88.38%	110.48%
FPC Duluth	Minimum	80.00%	88.35%	110.44%
FPC Eglin	Minimum	80.00%	84.80%	106.00%
FPC Alderson	Minimum	80.00%	81.37%	101.71%
FCI Lompoc	Low	70.00%	87.84%	125.49%
FCI Beaumont	Low	70.00%	84.11%	120.16%
FCI Safford	Low	70.00%	82.38%	117.69%
FCI Waseca	Low	70.00%	81.92%	117.03%
FCI Seagoville	Low	70.00%	80.60%	115.14%
FCI Danbury	Low	70.00%	75.85%	108.36%
FCI Texarkana	Low	70.00%	74.80%	106.86%
FCI Milan	Low	70.00%	74.74%	106.77%
FCI Tallahassee	Low	70.00%	74.55%	106.50%
FCI Bastrop	Low	70.00%	74.60%	105.80%
FCI Big Spring	Low	70.00%	71.58%	102.26%
FCI Coleman	Low	70.00%	70.66%	100.94%
FCI Dublin	Low	70.00%	68.20%	97.43%
FCI Elkton	Low	70.00%	67.85%	96.93%
FCI Fort Dix	Low	70.00%	67.76%	96.80%
FCI Sandstone	Low	70.00%	66.67%	95.24%
FCI La Tuna	Low	70.00%	65.77%	93.96%
FCI Forrest City	Low	70.00%	65.58%	93.69%
FCI Ashland	Low	70.00%	63.69%	90.99%
FCI Allenwood	Low	70.00%	61.36%	87.66%
FCI Yazoo City	Low	70.00%	60.53%	86.47%
FCI Butner	Low	70.00%	59.78%	85.40%
FCI Loretto	Low	70.00%	58.00%	82.86%
FCI Petersburg	Low	70.00%	55.61%	79.44%
FCI Phoenix	Medium	65.00%	88.51%	136.17%
FCI Florence	Medium	65.00%	82.72%	127.26%

[93] The BOP has not established CCC utilization goals for its high security institutions.

[94] The percentage of goal achieved is equal to the outcome divided by the goal.

CCC Utilization Goals and Outcomes FY 2001

Institution	Security Level	Goal[93]	Outcome	Percent of CCC Utilization Goal Achieved[94]
FCI Otisville	Medium	65.00%	82.67%	127.18%
FCI McKean	Medium	65.00%	80.43%	123.74%
FCI Cumberland	Medium	65.00%	77.94%	119.91%
FCI Oxford	Medium	65.00%	77.44%	119.14%
FCI Estill	Medium	65.00%	76.87%	118.26%
FCI Marianna	Medium	65.00%	74.74%	114.98%
FCI Butner	Medium	65.00%	74.27%	114.26%
FCI Coleman	Medium	65.00%	72.22%	111.11%
FCI Fairton	Medium	65.00%	72.02%	110.80%
FCI Pekin	Medium	65.00%	71.77%	110.42%
FCI Greenville	Medium	65.00%	70.69%	108.75%
FCI Jesup	Medium	65.00%	69.70%	107.23%
FCI Victorville	Medium	65.00%	69.64%	107.14%
FCI Terminal Island	Medium	65.00%	69.19%	106.45%
FCI Talladega	Medium	65.00%	69.11%	106.32%
FCI El Reno	Medium	65.00%	69.01%	106.17%
FCI Memphis	Medium	65.00%	68.99%	106.14%
FCI Sheridan	Medium	65.00%	68.88%	105.97%
FCI Beaumont	Medium	65.00%	67.50%	103.85%
FCI Beckley	Medium	65.00%	67.19%	103.37%
FCI Manchester	Medium	65.00%	66.91%	102.94%
FCI Allenwood	Medium	65.00%	65.52%	100.80%
FCI Englewood	Medium	65.00%	65.00%	100.00%
FCI Oakdale	Medium	65.00%	64.71%	99.55%
FCI Schuylkill	Medium	65.00%	62.39%	95.98%
FCI Tucson	Medium	65.00%	62.33%	95.89%
FCI Ray Brook	Medium	65.00%	59.56%	91.63%
FCI Miami	Medium	65.00%	59.21%	91.09%
FCI Edgefield	Medium	65.00%	57.53%	88.51%
FCI Three Rivers	Medium	65.00%	53.85%	82.85%
FCI Petersburg	Medium	65.00%	N/A	------
USP Leavenworth	High	N/A	56.25%	N/A
USP Terre Haute	High	N/A	48.28%	N/A
USP Lewisburg	High	N/A	42.42%	N/A
USP Beaumont	High	N/A	40.00%	N/A
USP Allenwood	High	N/A	36.84%	N/A
USP Marion	High	N/A	33.33%	N/A
USP Lompoc	High	N/A	27.59%	N/A
USP Atlanta	High	N/A	5.88%	N/A
USP Coleman	High	N/A	0.00%	N/A
USP Florence	High	N/A	0.00%	N/A
USP Pollock	High	N/A	0.00%	N/A
USP Atwater	High	N/A	N/A	------

CCC Utilization Goals and Outcomes FY 2001

Institution	Security Level	Goal[93]	Outcome	Percent of CCC Utilization Goal Achieved[94]
USP Lee	High	N/A	N/A	------
ADX Florence	Maximum	N/A	N/A[95]	------

---

[95] No inmates were released directly to the community from ADX Florence.

CCC Utilization Goals and Outcomes FY 2002

Institution	Security Level	Goal[96]	Outcome	Percent of CCC Utilization Goal Achieved[97]
FPC Nellis	Minimum	80.00%	95.96%	119.95%
FPC Pensacola	Minimum	80.00%	94.34%	117.93%
FPC Duluth	Minimum	80.00%	92.59%	115.74%
FPC Yankton	Minimum	80.00%	92.39%	115.49%
FPC Bryan	Minimum	80.00%	91.63%	114.54%
FPC Eglin	Minimum	80.00%	90.00%	112.50%
FPC Montgomery	Minimum	80.00%	89.17%	111.46%
FPC Allenwood	Minimum	80.00%	86.59%	108.24%
FCI Morgantown	Minimum	80.00%	85.19%	106.49%
FPC Seymour Johnson	Minimum	80.00%	80.69%	100.86%
FPC Alderson	Minimum	80.00%	80.27%	100.34%
FCI Seagoville	Low	70.00%	83.33%	119.04%
FCI Safford	Low	70.00%	82.86%	118.37%
FCI Lompoc	Low	70.00%	82.21%	117.44%
FCI Waseca	Low	70.00%	82.03%	117.19%
FCI Beaumont	Low	70.00%	81.99%	117.13%
FCI Milan	Low	70.00%	79.27%	113.24%
FCI Coleman	Low	70.00%	78.14%	111.63%
FCI Tallahassee	Low	70.00%	77.54%	110.77%
FCI Bastrop	Low	70.00%	75.62%	108.03%
FCI Danbury	Low	70.00%	75.43%	107.76%
FCI Forrest City	Low	70.00%	73.58%	105.11%
FCI Texarkana	Low	70.00%	73.20%	104.57%
FCI Yazoo City	Low	70.00%	68.31%	97.59%
FCI Ashland	Low	70.00%	68.26%	97.51%
FCI Dublin	Low	70.00%	67.40%	96.29%
FCI Big Spring	Low	70.00%	65.55%	93.64%
FCI Sandstone	Low	70.00%	64.84%	92.63%
FCI Loretto	Low	70.00%	64.21%	91.73%
FCI Elkton	Low	70.00%	63.18%	90.26%
FCI La Tuna	Low	70.00%	63.02%	90.03%
FCI Fort Dix	Low	70.00%	61.54%	87.91%
FCI Petersburg	Low	70.00%	55.34%	79.06%
FCI Butner	Low	70.00%	55.25%	78.93%
FCI Allenwood	Low	70.00%	51.97%	74.24%
FCI Oxford	Medium	65.00%	87.70%	134.92%
FCI Florence	Medium	65.00%	78.91%	121.40%
FCI Marianna	Medium	65.00%	78.57%	120.88%

[96] The BOP has not established CCC utilization goals for its high security institutions.

[97] The percentage of goal achieved is equal to the outcome divided by the goal.

CCC Utilization Goals and Outcomes FY 2002

Institution	Security Level	Goal[96]	Outcome	Percent of CCC Utilization Goal Achieved[97]
FCI Phoenix	Medium	65.00%	78.02%	120.03%
FCI Terminal Island	Medium	65.00%	77.23%	118.82%
FCI Sheridan	Medium	65.00%	76.95%	118.38%
FCI Schuylkill	Medium	65.00%	74.68%	114.89%
FCI Victorville	Medium	65.00%	72.87%	112.11%
FCI McKean	Medium	65.00%	72.83%	112.05%
FCI Talladega	Medium	65.00%	72.06%	110.86%
FCI Cumberland	Medium	65.00%	69.19%	106.45%
FCI El Reno	Medium	65.00%	67.82%	104.34%
FCI Manchester	Medium	65.00%	67.57%	103.95%
FCI Jesup	Medium	65.00%	67.55%	103.92%
FCI Tucson	Medium	65.00%	66.67%	102.57%
FCI Greenville	Medium	65.00%	65.57%	100.88%
FCI Miami	Medium	65.00%	65.52%	100.80%
FCI Butner	Medium	65.00%	65.43%	100.66%
FCI Estill	Medium	65.00%	64.75%	99.62%
FCI Coleman	Medium	65.00%	64.39%	99.06%
FCI Otisville	Medium	65.00%	63.06%	97.02%
FCI Pekin	Medium	65.00%	62.99%	96.91%
FCI Memphis	Medium	65.00%	62.76%	96.55%
FCI Beckley	Medium	65.00%	62.70%	96.46%
FCI Fairton	Medium	65.00%	62.27%	95.80%
FCI Beaumont	Medium	65.00%	59.50%	91.54%
FCI Oakdale	Medium	65.00%	57.26%	88.09%
FCI Ray Brook	Medium	65.00%	52.33%	80.51%
FCI Three Rivers	Medium	65.00%	50.89%	78.29%
FCI Allenwood	Medium	65.00%	49.54%	76.22%
FCI Edgefield	Medium	65.00%	42.00%	64.62%
FCI Petersburg	Medium	65.00%	41.18%	63.35%
FCI Englewood	Medium	65.00%	35.00%	53.85%
USP Atwater	High	N/A	75.00%	N/A
USP Lompoc	High	N/A	62.07%	N/A
USP Terre Haute	High	N/A	58.82%	N/A
USP Beaumont	High	N/A	58.00%	N/A
USP Leavenworth	High	N/A	53.23%	N/A
USP Marion	High	N/A	50.00%	N/A
USP Florence	High	N/A	45.28%	N/A
USP Allenwood	High	N/A	43.33%	N/A
USP Coleman	High	N/A	36.36%	N/A
USP Lewisburg	High	N/A	27.50%	N/A
USP Pollock	High	N/A	15.79%	N/A
USP Atlanta	High	N/A	15.45%	N/A
USP Lee	High	N/A	0.00%	N/A

CCC Utilization Goals and Outcomes FY 2002

Institution	Security Level	Goal[96]	Outcome	Percent of CCC Utilization Goal Achieved[97]
ADX Florence	Maximum	N/A	N/A[98]	------

---

[98] No inmates were released directly to the community from ADX Florence.

U.S. Department of Justice

Federal Bureau of Prisons

Office of the Director   _Washington, DC 20534_
                                            March 3, 2004

MEMORANDUM FOR GUY K. ZIMMERMAN
                ASSISTANT INSPECTOR GENERAL FOR AUDIT
                OFFICE OF INSPECTOR GENERAL

FROM: Harley G. Lappin, Director
                Federal Bureau of Prisons

SUBJECT: Response to the Office of Inspector General's
                (OIG) Draft Report: The Federal Bureau of Prisons
                Inmate Release Preparation and Transitional
                Reentry Programs

The Bureau of Prisons (BOP) appreciates the opportunity to
respond to the recommendations from the OIG's draft report The
Federal Bureau of Prisons Inmate Release Preparation and
Transitional Reentry Programs.

The Bureau has always taken great pride in our programs and
efforts to assist prisoners to reenter their communities
successfully and remain crime free. We consider this to be one
of our foremost programs of importance, within the confines of
creating a sound correctional environment that is both safe and
secure for prisoners, staff, and the community. We stress the
significance of this role in both our Mission and Vision
Statements.

I am particularly proud of our accomplishments with respect to
the Bureau's release preparation and reentry programs.
Furthermore, I believe the Bureau envisioned the need to continue
to enhance and refine our programs and initiatives in this arena
and has taken appropriate and well-defined steps in this regard.
As noted in your report, the Bureau's Executive Staff appointed a
reengineering team in May 2000 to examine our programs and

efforts with respect to developing inmate skills for successful reentry. The ideas and recommendations of this team are just beginning to come to fruition, and we are extremely pleased with the direction we are headed.

One of the most significant initiatives the Bureau has recently undertaken is the establishment of our Inmate Skills Development Branch in June 2003. The cornerstone of this initiative is the development of a multi-tiered process. This process includes an assessment tool, a skills development plan, programs within the institution, and community transition. The Inmate Skills Assessment Tool is used to accurately evaluate the inmate's reentry needs/deficits and abilities. This tool allows institution staff to prepare a comprehensive and individualized Skills Development Plan. Institution programs are used to target specific inmate needs, focus on skills acquisition, and reach high risk populations. Community transition, traditionally focused on the months preceding an inmate's release, is now expanded to include interagency communication and information sharing throughout the inmate's incarceration. Reentry skills are now a point of focus from initial designation to the successful transition back to the community.

Additionally, we have been working on several initiatives to improve the performance of our educational program offerings. The Bureau's preferred approach is to establish educational goals that are both challenging and realistic with the understanding that missed goals are not the only indicator of program failure. We are currently involved in a comprehensive effort to establish, monitor, and enforce educational goals. Our efforts include an increased focus on the accountability that truly determines the success of Bureau educational programs.

The Bureau, at all levels of the organization, has worked systematically and successfully to establish an effective strategic management system. Many of your findings and recommendations were items we self-identified and reported to your auditors that we were actively addressing.

I remain very proud of the efforts of Bureau staff in creating programs and an environment to assist inmates in successfully reentering their communities. I am confident we will continue to excel in providing inmates the appropriate programs and necessary skills and tools they need to remain crime free.

Our responses to your recommendations are as follows:

2

Recommendation #1: Ensure that a formalized process is established to set realistic occupational and educational completion goals stated as a percentage of completions to account for total enrollments and inmate population. The factors considered in setting educational goals should include the security level of the institution, inmate population, classroom size, number of classes, number of instructors, whether the institution has a wait list for its programs, and historical educational program completion data.

Response: The Bureau agrees with this recommendation. The Bureau will develop a formalized process to set realistic occupational and educational completion goals. The goals will be stated as a percentage of completions to account for total enrollments and inmate population. A target date of October 2006 has been established for implementation.

Recommendation #2: Establish and implement a formal process to ensure that institutions are held accountable for meeting their occupational and educational goals and that corrective action plans are developed to remedy performance so that goals are met in future years.

Response: The Bureau agrees with this recommendation. The Bureau will establish a formal process of accountability for institutions in meeting their occupational and educational goals. Corrective action plans will be developed as needed to remedy performance issues. A target date of October 2006 has been established for implementation.

Recommendation #3: Revise the Annual Program Report for Education and Recreation Services to include both the occupational and educational goals and outcomes for the reported fiscal year so that the BOP can readily determine whether the institution met its goals.

Response: The Bureau agrees with this recommendation. The Bureau revised the Annual Program Report for Education and Recreation Services in FY 2003 to include both the occupational and educational goals and outcomes for the reported fiscal year. Attached is copy of the revised report. (See Attachment A)

Recommendation #4: Establish and implement a formal standardized process for evaluating the performance factor for occupational, technical, and vocational programs on an annual basis to ensure that the BOP institutions are held accountable for low performance and that corrective action plans are developed to remedy occupational program performance.

3

Response: The Bureau agrees with this recommendation. Using the results of recommendations #1 and #2, the Bureau will implement a formal standardized process for annually evaluating institutions' performance and accountability. Corrective action plans will be developed to remedy occupational program performance. The target date of October 2006 has been established for implementation.

Recommendation #5: Ensure that a formal standardized process is developed and implemented to screen all inmates prior to enrollment in all occupational programs to ensure that they have the ability and are willing to commit to completing the course.

Response: The Bureau agrees with this recommendation. We are currently piloting procedures for assessing the occupational needs of inmates. Additionally, we are making contact with State correctional agencies to assess additional procedures used to screen eligibility for occupational programs. The results of this assessment will be used to establish a protocol involving several components, such as criteria for structured interviews and document reviews to address inmate needs, abilities, and interest in completing programs. A target date of January 2006 has been established for implementation.

Recommendation #6: Ensure that a suitable measure of literacy program performance is developed to evaluate its institutions. The new performance measure should provide an accurate picture of the percentage of all inmates that arrive at the BOP institutions without a GED credential or high school diploma who complete the literacy program during incarceration.

Response: The Bureau agrees with this recommendation. The Bureau is revising policy to incorporate these changes. This revision will require rules language changes. The new data procedures will allow us to obtain an accurate picture of the percentage of all inmates, entering the Bureau after the implementation date of the new policy, who lack a GED or high school diploma and their GED status upon release. This will allow us to determine which inmates, releasing from the Bureau with a GED, actually earned the GED while incarcerated. A target date of September 2007 has been established for implementation.

Recommendation #7: Ensure that the percentage of citizen inmates required to participate in the literacy program that have dropped out at each institution is more closely evaluated.

Response: The Bureau agrees with this recommendation. The Bureau will create a performance measurement for the percentage of citizen inmates with needs who have dropped out of the

4

literacy program at the national and regional level. We will incorporate this measure into monthly reports to allow monitoring of each institution. A target date of March 2005 has been established for implementation.

Recommendation #8: Ensure that the percentage of non-citizen inmates that have dropped out of the literacy program at each institution is monitored.

Response: The Bureau agrees with this recommendation. The Bureau will create a performance measurement for the percentage of non-citizen inmates with needs who have dropped out of the literacy program at the national and regional level. We will incorporate this measure into monthly reports to allow monitoring of each institution. A target date of September 2005 has been established for implementation.

Recommendation #9: Establish and implement a mechanism to hold institutions accountable for the monthly psychological program participation data that includes corrective action plans for institutions with low participation.

Response: The Bureau agrees with this recommendation. The Bureau will develop a system for reporting on program resources and participation. Institutions will report to the region each month on the utilization of allocated positions and the participation indicators for each Psychology Treatment Program, including Residential Drug Abuse Programs (RDAP). Quarterly, each region will report to the Central Office on program performance measures. If a program falls below 90% participation for the quarter, the region will develop a corrective action plan. Psychology Program Utilization Data will be included in the Key Indicators System. A target date of October 2004 has been established for implementation.

Recommendation #10: Ensure that participation data is tracked for all of the BOP institutions to determine the percentage of eligible inmates that have completed the RPP prior to release into the community.

Response: The Bureau agrees with this recommendation. As discussed during the exit conference, the new Inmate Skills initiative will focus on community transition throughout the inmate's incarceration and will better assist their successful reentry. Therefore, based on this information, your staff agreed to close recommendations 10 and 11.

5

Recommendation #11: Establish and implement a mechanism to hold institutions accountable for RPP performance that includes corrective action plans for institutions with low performance.

Response: The Bureau agrees with this recommendation. As discussed during the exit conference, the new Inmate Skills initiative will focus on community transition throughout the inmate's incarceration and will better assist their successful reentry. Therefore, based on this information, your staff agreed to close recommendations 10 and 11.

Recommendation #12: Establish a CCC utilization target for its high security institutions.

Response: The Bureau agrees with this recommendation. The Bureau has established a 65% target CCC utilization rate for high security institutions. This was added to the Bureau's Strategic Plan February 4, 2004. (See Attachment B)

Recommendation #13: Establish and implement a formal process to ensure that all eligible inmates are placed in a CCC prior to release.

Response: The Bureau agrees with this recommendation. The Bureau will implement a formal process for reviewing eligible inmates that are denied or not referred for CCC placement. The process will be initiated at the institution level and include regional review for compliance with national policy. A target date of July 30, 2004, has been established for implementation.

If you have any questions regarding this response, please contact Michael W. Garrett, Senior Deputy Assistant Director, Program Review Division, at (202) 616-2099.

Attachments

6

ANALYSIS AND SUMMARY OF ACTIONS
NECESSARY TO CLOSE THE REPORT

The BOP response to the audit (Appendix XIV) describes the actions taken or planned to implement our recommendations. Our analysis of the BOP's response to specific recommendations is provided below. In addition to responding to the recommendations, the BOP made several claims in the program overview section of its response to which we first respond.

The BOP states in its response to the draft report that the establishment of the Inmate Skills Development Branch in June 2003 is one of the most significant initiatives related to the preparation of inmates for successful transition into the community. As stated in the background section of our report, the mission of the Inmate Skills Development Branch is to "coordinate the [BOP's] efforts to implement inmate skill development initiatives and provide a centralized point of liaison with external agencies to equip inmates with the necessary skills to succeed upon release." However, it is important to note that, at this time, we are unable to determine what impact, if any, the initiative will have on the issues identified in this report because the Inmate Skills Development Branch is still in its developmental stage.

The BOP also states in its response to the draft report that, "Many of your findings and recommendations were items we self-identified and reported to your auditors that we were actively addressing." In our judgment, this statement is somewhat misleading. While it may be true that the BOP was aware of some of the findings included in our report, much of this information was not shared with the auditors until our preliminary findings were presented to BOP officials.

1. **Resolved.** This recommendation can be closed when we receive documentation supporting that the BOP has implemented a formal process to set realistic occupational and educational program goals stated as a percentage of completions to account for total enrollments and the inmate population.

2. **Resolved.** This recommendation can be closed when we receive documentation supporting that the BOP has implemented a formal process of accountability for institutions in meeting their occupational and educational program completion goals that includes corrective action plans, as necessary, to remedy performance issues.

3.   **Closed.**

4.   **Resolved.** This recommendation can be closed when we receive documentation supporting that the BOP has implemented a formal standard process for evaluating institutions' occupational program performance and accountability annually that includes corrective action plans, as necessary, to remedy program performance.

5.   **Resolved.** This recommendation can be closed when we receive documentation supporting that the BOP has implemented procedures for assessing the occupational needs of inmates and a formal standard process for screening inmates prior to enrollment in an occupational program.

6.   **Resolved.** This recommendation can be closed when we receive documentation supporting that the BOP has implemented new data collection procedures that provide an accurate picture of the percentage of all inmates entering BOP institutions who lack a high school diploma or GED and the percentage of those inmates who actually earn a GED while incarcerated in a BOP institution.

7.   **Resolved.** This recommendation can be closed when we receive documentation supporting that the BOP has implemented a performance measurement for the percentage of citizen inmates with GED needs who have dropped out of the literacy program at the national and regional level and incorporated the measure into monthly reports for monitoring performance at each institution.

8.   **Resolved.** This recommendation can be closed when we receive documentation supporting that the BOP has implemented a performance measurement for the percentage of noncitizen inmates with GED needs who have dropped out of the literacy program at the national and regional level and incorporated the measure into monthly reports for monitoring performance at each institution.

9.   **Resolved.** This recommendation can be closed when we receive documentation supporting that the BOP has implemented a system for reporting on psychological program resources and participation that includes developing corrective action plans if program participation falls below 90 percent.

10. **Resolved.** The BOP states in its response to the draft report that during the exit conference the auditors agreed to close recommendations 10 and 11 based on information provided during the exit conference related to the BOP's plans to eliminate the RPP once the Inmate Skills initiative is fully implemented. Rather, the auditors stated that if the RPP was eliminated, recommendations 10 and 11 could be closed; however, we did not agree to close the recommendations at this time. This recommendation can be closed when we receive documentation supporting that the BOP has eliminated the RPP and fully implemented the Inmate Skills initiative which focuses on community transition throughout the inmate's incarceration.

11. **Resolved.** This recommendation can be closed when we receive documentation supporting that the BOP has eliminated the RPP and fully implemented the Inmate Skills initiative which focuses on community transition throughout the inmate's incarceration.

12. **Closed.**

13. **Resolved.** This recommendation can be closed when we receive documentation supporting that the BOP has implemented a formal process for reviewing eligible inmates that are denied or not referred for CCC placement that includes region review for compliance with national policy.

www.ingramcontent.com/pod-product-compliance
Lightning Source LLC
Chambersburg PA
CBHW081352280526
45788CB00009B/2857